MW00574358

CRAFT ARTISTS

PRACTICAL CAREER GUIDES

Series Editor: Kezia Endsley

Computer Game Development & Animation, by Tracy Brown Hamilton
Craft Artists, by Marcia Santore
Culinary Arts, by Tracy Brown Hamilton
Dental Assistants and Hygienists, by Kezia Endsley
Education Professionals, by Kezia Endsley
Fine Artists, by Marcia Santore
First Responders, by Kezia Endsley
Health and Fitness Professionals, by Kezia Endsley
Information Technology (IT) Professionals, by Erik Dafforn
Medical Office Professionals, by Marcia Santore
Skilled Trade Professionals, by Corbin Collins

CRAFT ARTISTS

A Practical Career Guide

MARCIA SANTORE

ROWMAN & LITTLEFIELD

Lanham • Boulder • New York • London

Published by Rowman & Littlefield
An imprint of The Rowman & Littlefield Publishing Group, Inc.
4501 Forbes Boulevard, Suite 200, Lanham, Maryland 20706
www.rowman.com

6 Tinworth Street, London, SE11 5AL, United Kingdom

British Library Cataloguing in Publication Information Available

Library of Congress Cataloging-in-Publication Data

Names: Santore, Marcia, 1960–author.
Title: Craft artists : a practical career guide / Marcia Santore.
Description: Lanham : Rowman & Littlefield, [2020] | Series: Practical
  career guides | Includes bibliographical references. | Summary: "Craft
  Artists: A Practical Career Guide includes interviews with professionals
  in the following fields. Tattoo Artists; Ceramic Artists; Glass blowers;
  Blacksmiths; Jewelers; Woodworkers"— Provided by publisher.
Identifiers: LCCN 2019038957 (print) | LCCN 2019038958 (ebook) | ISBN
  9781538134306 (paperback) | ISBN 9781538134313 (epub)
Subjects: LCSH: Handicraft—Vocational guidance. | Decorative
  arts—Vocational guidance.
Classification: LCC TT149 .S36 2020 (print) | LCC TT149 (ebook) | DDC
  745.5023—dc23
LC record available at https://lccn.loc.gov/2019038957
LC ebook record available at https://lccn.loc.gov/2019038958

Contents

Introduction

Being a craft artist means making things that are both beautiful and useful.
Studio-Annika/Getty Images

Welcome to a Career in Craft Art!

Craft artists have the joy of creating beautiful, well made, aesthetically pleasing objects that are also useful. Craft artists may be small businesspersons or may work for small or large companies. If you love to work with your hands and create unique things, then craft art may be for you.

> There is something deeply satisfying in shaping something with your hands. Proper artificing is like a song made solid. It is an act of creation.—Patrick Rothfuss[1]

What Is a Craft Artist?

A craft artist—or artisan—is someone who makes one-of-a-kind, unique objects that are beautifully constructed by hand. The term "craft" implies something that is well made by hand, has a use beyond an aesthetic one, is unique or made in small quantities, and is more special than something produced in a factory.

Craft artists primarily use natural materials—such as wood, clay, fiber, metal, or foodstuffs—and turn them into useful and unique things. Some crafts are taught in art schools or college and university art departments; others are learned by working with a master artisan to learn the techniques, rules, traditions, and business of that particular craft.

Creativity is very important to a career as a craft artist, but it takes more than good ideas. It takes knowledge of your craft and what others who are pursuing it are doing to move the craft forward. Many people begin a craft art career as a hobby. In order to be good enough at your craft to do it professionally, you'll need to work hard to develop and improve your skills, to understand your materials, and know what others are accomplishing in the same craft. You'll also need to understand your business, and to develop a workable plan to build a clientele and market your finished products.

What Is Craftsmanship?

The term "craftsmanship" speaks to skill in a particular craft, to the quality of the design and work in an object that is made by hand by someone who knows what they're doing. Of course, the term "craftsman" also refers to women, so "craftsperson" and "artisan" may both be better terms to use when talking

> Craftsmanship is the quality that comes from creating with passion, care, and attention to detail. It is a quality that is honed, refined, and practiced over the course of a career.—Richard Glover[2]

about people. But the concept of "craftsmanship" as a mark of quality is so well established that the term continues to be used to mean both men and women.

According to Todd Oppenheimer and his team at the Craftsmanship Initiative,

> At its base, the term craftsmanship describes an object that has been made with the highest quality, by someone who fully understands the materials and techniques involved. On a higher level, craftsmanship is defined by the values that such work requires, such as precision, integrity, and durability—today more often called sustainability. These principles apply to any pursuit, from fashion to farming, from film to physics.[3]

No matter what career you end up pursuing, the qualities that define craftsmanship will serve you well.

Craft Artist Careers

There are so many different possible craft options that we can't possibly cover them all here—check out the following sidebar to see just some of the many options. In this book, we'll meet six artisans and talk about careers in the craft arts from the point of view of their particular crafts. These are all professional craft artists who make most or all of their living from their craft arts businesses.

Can You Make a Living as an Artisan?

Yes! All the artisans in this book are doing just that. Craft artist careers require focus and dedication. Depending on the craft you pursue, if you are dedicated to making it your career and are willing to put in the hard work it takes to build your business, you can make a living doing what you love.

Few craft artists actually become wealthy and it can be hard to make ends meet, especially while you're establishing yourself. Some craft artists find they also want to supplement their income or expand their horizons by taking on an additional job from time to time or on a regular basis. We'll talk more about that in chapter 2.

WHAT DO ARTISANS MAKE?

Baking
Basketry
Botanicals
Brewing
Calligraphy
Ceramics
Fabric and textile crafts
- Accessories design
- Canvas work
- Clothing design
- Crochet
- Embroidery
- Felting
- Knitting
- Lacemaking
- Macramé
- Paracord
- Quilting
- Ropemaking
- Rug hooking
- Rug making
- Shoe making
- Spinning
- Stitching
- Tatting
- Weaving
Floral
Glass art
- Blown
- Fused
Jewelry
- Beading
- Cloisonné enamel

- Keum-boo
- Metal
- Nonmetal
Landscape design
Leatherwork
Metal crafts
- Blacksmithing
- Casting
- Clockmaking
- Coppersmithing
- Enameling
- Engraving
- Farrier
- Goldsmithing
- Jewelery
- Knife making
- Lapidary
- Locksmithing
- Metal casting
- Metalsmithing
- Pewter
- Silversmithing
- Tinsmithing
- Watchmaking
- Weaponsmith (sword making, armorer, gunsmith, fletcher)
Needlework
- Appliqué
- Crewel embroidery
- Crochet
- Cross-stitch
- Embroidery
- Ribbon embroidery

- Knitting
- Needlepoint
- Patchwork
- Quilting

Paper crafts
- Bookbinding
- Calligraphy
- Cast paper
- Decoupage
- Iris folding
- Origami (paper folding)
- Paper embossing
- Paper marbling
- Paper model
- Papercutting
- Papermaking
- Papier-mâché
- Parchment craft
- Quilling

Stone crafts
- Flintknapping
- Letter carving on stone
- Mosaics and inlaying
- Stone carving
- Stonemasonry

Tattoo art

Taxidermy

Wood and furniture crafts
- Cabinetmaking
- Carpentry
- Intarsia
- Lacquer art
- Marquetry
- Upholstery
- Wood burning
- Wood carving
- Woodturning
- Woodworking

The Artisan Personality

Basing his work on the ancient Greek philosopher Plato and physician Hippocrates, psychologist David Keirsey (1921–2013) came up with a personality test that groups people into four temperaments. While Keirsey was organizing people in general, what he had to say about the artisan temperament applies to many actual artisans.

Does this description strike a chord with you?

Artisans are most at home in the real world of solid objects that can be made and manipulated, and of real-life events that can be experienced in the here and now. Artisans have exceptionally keen senses, and love working with their hands. They seem right at home with tools, instruments, and vehicles of all kinds, and their actions are usually aimed at getting them where they want to go, and as quickly as possible. Thus Artisans will strike off boldly down roads that others might consider risky or impossible, doing whatever it takes, rules or no rules, to accomplish their goals.[4]

Why Choose a Career in Craft Arts?

Craft artists have the joy and satisfaction of making something useful with their own hands.
Jgalione/E+/Getty Images

Being a Craft Artist or Artisan

*A*s the craft artists you'll meet in this book all agree, being an artisan is more than a job—it's a lifestyle. As a craftsperson, you will spend a lifetime building, improving, and honing your skills in the service of your creative ideas. You will be an entrepreneur, running your own business and working collaboratively with customers to create something new in the world that is useful and unique.

Creativity is simply the human brain forming new connections between ideas, and we all are engaged in this process every day. The common idea that there are some people who are creative and some who are not is a myth. On some level, we are all artists. We are all creators.—Michael Gungor[1]

Characteristics of a Craft Artist

People who become successful as craft artists tend to have certain things in common. Artisans are people who have the talent and the skill to make useful things with their hands. But artisans are not just manufacturers. Artisans are dedicated to creating beautiful, interesting, or thought-provoking works that enhance people's lives.

Artisans need:

- *Creativity.* Creativity is the ability to make something new happen in the universe. Creativity is problem-solving, even if you can't (yet) define what the problem is. It means looking at things differently, considering many options, trying and discarding ideas, and then making something new out of all of it. Artisans don't want to just do the same thing over and over again. To be successful in your craft, you will want to be able to think up new ideas, solve new problems, and reach new goals.
- *Dexterity.* To make things with your hands, you need to be good with your hands and able to manipulate the tools and materials you use. To improve your dexterity, try slowing down and repeating a technique many times until it is safely stored in your body memory.
- *Artistic ability, usually in more than one medium.* For instance, if you want to be a jeweler or a knife maker or a woodworker, you need to develop the knowledge and skills for that particular craft. But you will also need to be able to draw in order to plan your creations.
- *Patience and persistence.* Patience doesn't mean sitting around waiting for opportunities to come to you. Patience means accepting that things take time, and that fretting and stressing about it doesn't make things happen any sooner. Patience means accepting that if one opportunity

doesn't work out, there is always another one. Some craft skills take years to truly master, so you will need patience to develop the skills you need to bring your ideas to life. Persistence is a skill you can develop. Check out the sidebar on how to develop your persistence!

- *Interpersonal skills.* Artisans deal with other people all the time. You'll need to be able to work well with customers, with clients who want to commission a piece, with your assistants and/or bosses, with the vendors who provide your materials, with stores, galleries, and other stockists.

- *Faith in yourself and your work.* Some people seem to be born confident or talented or both. Others need to develop it over the course of a lifetime. Faith in yourself and your work doesn't mean arrogance, or the assumption that you have nothing new or different to learn. It means an internal confidence in your ability to learn, to imagine, and to create that will carry you during difficult times. It means learning to recognize when your work is good. It also means being confident enough in your abilities to recognize when a piece is not working so that you can either fix it or set it aside and move on to something else.

- *Business skills.* Successful artisans understand their market (what their customers want and need), production costs, pricing, sales, marketing, and inventory management. We'll talk about this in detail in the last chapter of this book.

Craft Artist Careers

Of course, job prospects for craft artists vary depending on which craft you pursue. So we'll be talking about the specific craft careers that match the craft artists in this book. This will give you an overview of these careers as well as a general idea of the kind of information you could look for, if you're interested in a different craft or artisan career.

Since most professional craft artists are self-employed, it's hard to pinpoint things like annual income for these careers. The US Bureau of Labor Statistics (BLS) reports that craft and fine artists earned a median annual income of $48,960 in 2019 and predicts about 6 percent job growth by 2026 (about the national average). The BLS points out that "[e]mployment growth for artists

PERSISTENCE

Persistence means you keep going. As an artisan, you'll need persistence at every level, from learning skills to finishing work to developing your own style to creating a body of work to getting your work in front of people. Persistence means pushing forward when outside influences are pushing back.

The good news is that persistence is a skill that you can teach yourself. So how do you become persistent?

1. *Know your goals.* It's easier to keep moving if you can see where you're going.
2. *Keep your goals reachable.* How do you eat an elephant? One bite at a time. Don't frighten yourself with large, distant goals like "have a solo exhibition at the Museum of Modern Art in New York." Focus on the next thing you need to do—start a piece, finish a piece, turn an assignment in on time, etc.
3. *Know your priorities.* You already know what your priorities are. Get your schoolwork done. Get your work-work done. Hang with your friends. Call your mom. And make art. Not necessarily in that order.
4. *Make art a priority.* Make making art a priority in your life. Carve out time in your schedule for the studio.
5. *Use positive self-talk.* Don't let your inner voice give you a hard time. We all have a nasty little inner voice that makes us doubt ourselves. Sometimes your inner voice tells you to watch TV or play video games instead of making art. Counter that voice by purposely talking to yourself in a supportive and positive way. No, not out loud. Tell yourself, "I'm just going to do this now."
6. *Get in the habit of getting in the habit.* Pick a thing and do it. Then pick another thing and do that. Repeat.
7. *Notice when you finish.* Pay attention to those special times when you complete a project. Feel proud of yourself. See how nice that is? Noticing how good it feels to finish something helps you be persistent in the future.

depends largely on the overall state of the economy and whether people are willing to spend money on art, because people usually buy art when they can afford to do so."[2]

Craft artists generally work in their own studios. They sell their creations directly to customers through commissions and in venues like craft fairs and festivals. Craft artists also work with galleries and stores to stock their pieces for retail sales—this expands the artisan's reach to places around the country or around the world.

> There's a real ceramic renaissance happening in the last ten years. There's a return to craft—maybe as a response to the oversaturation of technology. We're out of touch with our hands and the earth.—Suzanne Wang, ceramic artist

CERAMICIST/POTTER

A ceramicist (ceramic artist or potter) makes objects out of clay. The term "ceramics" means things that are changed by heat, so that includes the glazes that are used to enhance or decorate the surface of ceramic pieces as well as the clay they are made of. Ceramic artists make unique objects that reflect their personal style, while production potters make large numbers of pieces that are intended to be all the same (such as plates, cups, and bowls of a particular pattern).

Ceramic artists typically work in a ceramics studio with tables, throwing wheels, shelves, and a kiln to fire the clay pieces when they are dry. Some like to purchase clay from a known vendor, while others like to dig their own clay out of the ground. Ceramic pieces can be built by hand or thrown on a potter's wheel; some production pottery pieces are made in plaster molds.

Ceramic artists have different options for learning their craft. Many art schools and college/university art departments offer ceramics as a major leading to a bachelor of fine arts (BFA) degree in studio art or ceramics. Many ceramic artists begin working with clay as early as elementary school, building their skills with classes at school, camp programs, community classes, workshops, and learning with local potters. Those interested in ceramics from a scientific or industrial point of view can earn degrees in ceramic engineering.

Ceramic artists get to play in the dirt. *LightFieldStudios/iStock/Getty Images*

SUZANNE WANG—CERAMIC ARTIST

Suzanne Wang.
Courtesy of Suzanne Wang

Suzanne Wang holds bachelor's and master's degrees in film and theater design. After a decade working in that field, she felt the call to return to clay and in 2015 apprenticed with master potter Ken Matsuzaki in Japan. Today, she lives on the Big Island of Hawaii and creates ceramic artworks inspired by the island's natural surroundings and multicultural society. Her work can be seen online at www.suzannewangceramics.com.

How did you become interested in ceramics?

I took it in high school—that was the first time I ever touched clay. I stopped doing it for about sixteen years and got degrees in other fields and worked in other industries before returning to it in my late thirties. I love that it's tactile and malleable. There's so much versatility with what you can do with it—you can make sculpture, functional ware, there's such a huge range to play with. Also, working in ceramics is a great teacher because you have to learn a lot about chemistry, about form and function, which brings you into food culture and tea—it can give you an education for your whole life.

What is a typical day on your job?

I'm a night person so I tend to relax in the morning, and I'll do preparation kinds of things or continue what I was working on the night before. I tend to start throwing in the afternoon and evening. Because I live in Hawaii, I like to use the sunshine to dry my pieces faster—I live in a pretty wet area. I really like evening as a time to work, because I don't have any distractions. Phones aren't ringing. People aren't stopping by.

What's the best part of your job?

Being my own boss and doing work that is about me finding my expression. It's really personal. It's not just one thing. I love the intimacy of making things people can use. There's a real humbleness and connectedness with my audience that I really love. I don't really have to deal with office politics and power struggles and personality differences, hierarchy. Working in ceramics, it's just me. But I'm not isolated, because I have to sell my work so I'm dealing with people directly—galleries and stores. I'm a social person, so that helps break up the periods of isolation.

What's the most challenging part of your job?

Making money. Maintaining self-discipline to keep the work slow, steady, and efficient.

What's the most surprising thing about your job?

I've met so many incredible people by working in pottery. Even though there are financial struggles, it's a world of abundance between people, customers, other potters. It's a very generous field to be working in.

Where and how do you sell your work?

I do four or five craft-related events per year, like the Hilo Orchid show, an annual makers' market, a holiday group pottery sale, and then I have two open studios a year. I periodically do trunk shows at the Four Seasons Hotel or the Volcano Art Center at the national park. I also sell my work through consignment or wholesale through galleries and stores. This year, I plan to open my online shop.

What would be your best tip on those interactions?

I think it's always good to first go to the store and see their products to see if your art works in that store or gallery. I don't believe in oversaturating my product—I like to be selective about where my work is shown. My work is a little pricier. It depends on what kind of work you make. If you're a production potter and your price point is lower, you can sell at farmer's markets. But if you want to be perceived as more of an artist, it's important to be selective. It's important to think about how you want to present yourself. It's good to find out who the contact person is and get their e-mail, and then introduce yourself in an e-mail with examples of your work. You *must* have a website. Sometimes it helps to include your Instagram feed. Then follow up with a phone call if they don't respond a week later.

Did your education prepare you for the job?

I have a bachelor's and master's in set design for theater and film from San Francisco State and NYU. I did a one-year apprenticeship with a master potter in Japan. Apprenticeship or interning is definitely a fast track into making a living as a potter. It may be more important than going to school for it. What happens in a class-room is totally different from trying to make a living. Working in a studio with a professional potter, you learn about the lifestyle. Because being a potter is not a job, it's a lifestyle. It has different challenges. You have to be really structured to be a potter. Timing is very important to pottery—firing schedules, glazing, drying, all these things have to be planned well in advance. You're constantly looking at your calendar, marking dates, setting goals. It's not a good field for someone who doesn't like to be a planner. It requires a lot of organizational skills, especially if you mix your own glazes, which serious potters do.

Is the job what you expected?

No! It wasn't until I apprenticed that I realized the scope of work involved in making a living doing this. I never would have understood that by going to school for it or just taking classes here and there. It's the hardest job I've ever had, but it's the most rewarding.

What's next, where do you see yourself going from here?

I'm still in the category of emerging artist, I'm not fully supporting myself the way I want to. I have to supplement my income with freelance work (about 70 percent of my income comes from pottery and 30 percent from design or other jobs).

A lot of potters end up being teachers to supplement their income. I teach kids once a week, we work on projects. I also teach workshops once or twice a year for adults at art centers. I enjoy people and I enjoy sharing, but it's really different from working at home. It's important to do to get myself out there, it's a great exercise. I like sharing the information. I put everything into it, so I have to be careful. I don't want teaching to take over my work. My teacher in Japan always said do one or the other, it's hard to do both without sacrificing and it's usually your art that's sacrificed. But for some people, they like that!

When I started the apprenticeship, I gave myself a five-year timeline to get everything together. I see myself as an artist and not just a craftsman. Not every ceramicist feels that way—there's such a broad range of what you can do. You can work in production pottery or industrial ceramic engineering or be a studio potter/ artist. One way to make more money is to be a fine artist and do more large pieces as home décor or corporate and hotel commissions. It's a little bit more commercial. I would like to do a little bit of that, but not be consumed by that. I still want to make items for the everyday person.

Where do you see the field going from here?

There's a real ceramic renaissance happening in the last ten years. There's a return to craft—maybe as a response to the oversaturation of technology. We're out of touch with our hands and the earth. Resources (clay, fuel) are getting more expensive. We're competing with the Ikeas that can produce things that look handmade but are actually mass-produced, cheap goods. But then you also have people with a lot of money now who can tell the difference and want to spend money on higher quality goods made by local artisans, so there is opportunity to make a living doing this.

How can a young person prepare for this career?

Keep taking classes in college and if you can get a summer internship, start that way. And if you really feel more serious about it, try to embark on a two-year apprenticeship with a master potter. Look for people whose work you like and contact them. Usually, you get paid very little but in exchange for the work you do, you get to make work and fire for free and get mentorship.

What's something you know now about running a ceramics business that you wish you'd known when you started out?

I wish I'd known how expensive it would be to set up the studio. If you live where I live in Hawaii, there aren't a lot of cooperatives where you can share the cost. That's a huge challenge for people. If you live on the mainland in a pottery center like Minnesota, North Carolina, or California, there are tons of places to take classes and get involved as a volunteer or apprentice. Research the region you live in and get to know who's there. New England has tons of woodfire potters, for instance. Potters are such nice people, very down to earth. There's a lot less ego than in some fields. It's not a problem to meet potters who are generous.

GLASS ARTIST

Contemporary glass artists use several different approaches to create their work. Hot glass techniques include glassblowing, sculpting, and casting in molds. Warm glass processes use a kiln to fuse glass or "slump" (bend) it, as well as another kind of molding called kiln casting. Cold glass processes include etching, sandblasting, grinding, polishing, and engraving. Stained glass and leaded glass both involve piecing together cut glass shapes into a design, held together with copper or lead.

In glassblowing, the artist gathers melted (molten) glass onto the end of a thin pipe, then blows in the other end of the pipe to make an air bubble inside the glass. By turning the pipe and pulling and pushing the molten glass with tools, the glass artist is able to create shapes.

Glassblowing requires careful training and practice because you are working with open fire and extremely hot melted glass. The furnace is heated to 2,000°F (1,090°C)! The glassblowing studio includes lots of specialized tools and equipment. There are a few schools that offer degrees or certificates in glassblowing. Most glass artists learn their trade from master glass artists while working as

Glassblowing requires care, skill, and practice. *Jgalione/E+/Getty Images*

assistants or apprentices. Glassblowing is difficult work, so most glass artists need assistants and apprentices, which is good for the novice glassblower.

Glass artists work in their own studios and create pieces they can sell to the public, directly or through stockists. In addition, glassblowers give live demonstrations of this traditional practice at living museums, glass museums, festivals, and fairs.

> I learned more about how to run a business in the six or seven years when I worked for other people. . . . That's where I picked up the practical experience to make it all work. . . . My first jobs were production work and that trained me to be efficient, so I didn't waste a lot of time and energy, which is key to keeping going.—Michael Hopko, glass artist

BLACKSMITH

Blacksmithing means "the art or process of shaping and forging metal with the use of heat and tools."[3] Throughout history, blacksmiths have made tools, weapons, nails, gates and fences, horseshoes, and everything else made from iron that was needed. Today, blacksmiths often create unique works of art that also serve necessary functions. In addition, television shows like *Forged in Fire* on the History Channel have made more people aware of blacksmithing and more eager to learn this traditional craft.

A forge is the fire where blacksmiths heat metal such as iron or steel until it is bendable. (The term "forge" is often used, as well, to mean the smithy, that is, the smith's workshop.)

There are (as of this writing) seventy-seven schools and colleges that teach blacksmithing listed on the Artist-Blacksmith's Association of North America (ABANA) website. These range from folk schools and craft centers to community colleges to universities. Yes, you can get a degree in blacksmithing. On the other hand, many of today's blacksmiths begin forging as a hobby. Those who want to progress as professional blacksmiths can apprentice under a master blacksmith, become a journeyman and eventually become master blacksmiths themselves. ABANA also provides a long list of regional blacksmith groups,

Blacksmiths create beautiful and unique pieces on commission for clients.
ilbusca/E+/Getty Images

where you can meet professional blacksmiths, attend workshops and demonstrations, and learn about the life and the craft.

There are many different ways to earn a living in metalwork and blacksmiths are needed in many industrial area of manufacturing and transportation. As craft artists, blacksmiths demonstrate techniques at living museums, fairs, festivals, and workshops; create metal sculptures; and teach blacksmithing to others. Farriers (who are responsible for the care of horses' hooves) also need blacksmithing skills to create custom-fitted horseshoes. Many blacksmiths work out of their own smithy directly with clients who commission special, unique pieces—from elaborate iron gates to impeccable chef's knives.

I've had clients that have been more than willing to let me do my thing with minimal input—they want my thing, my style. People end up recognizing my work somewhere, because of my style, and that's pretty neat.—Sue Howerter, blacksmith

WOODWORKER

Woodworking includes everything from building furniture to building custom cabinets to finish carpentry to wood sculptures to toys to delicate inlay work. Many people enjoy making things from wood—building birdhouses or simple furniture or turning wood on a lathe. Professional woodworkers perfect their skills in all woodworking techniques, including the safe use of hand and power tools, as well as close attention to detail. They must also understand how to stain, seal, and otherwise protect the wood to protect it over time.

Woodworking can be learned in shop classes or from someone (professional or not) who knows how to do it. There are also degree or certificate programs in woodworking, carpentry, or cabinetmaking from community and technical colleges. Apprenticing with a master woodworker helps complete your education, while building your woodworking and business skills.

Precision is extremely important in creating furniture or cabinetry, so a craft artist working in wood needs to have good math skills and the patience to be sure that every cut is correct and every joint perfectly aligned. (There is a fine old saying in carpentry: measure twice, cut once!) Taking your time with every aspect of woodworking will also help keep you from getting hurt. As Liz Grace

Working with wood. *Geber86/E+/Getty Images*

(see chapter 4) tells her students, "I want you to leave with the same number of body parts you came in with."

Some woodworkers support themselves by doing rough or finish carpentry for construction projects as well as working with clients who commission unique pieces of furniture. Others focus on a particular type of woodworking, perhaps specializing in toys, smaller household items, re-creating building details and millwork, or creating a certain style of furniture.

> I was surprised and pleased to find how willing other woodworkers are to share their knowledge and skills with someone just starting out. I've found that wood-workers are very open, generous, giving of their time. They're noncompetitive in that way.—Liz Grace, woodworker

TATTOO ARTIST

Tattoo artists use ink, needles, and their own design and drawing skills to embed permanent artwork into their clients' skin. It requires technique, practice, patience, and people skills to bring a customer's innermost feelings into pictorial form on their bodies. The customer must be able to trust the tattoo artist absolutely.

Up until the early part of the twenty-first century, tattooing was illegal in many states because it was seen as a threat to public health. As states developed licensing standards, including standards for clean, sterile equipment and work environments, tattooing is now legal in all fifty states. State laws regulate things like health and cleanliness, licensing, and client age (generally, nobody under age eighteen can legally be tattooed because they are not old enough to enter into a legal contract).

The primary way to learn tattooing is through an apprenticeship. Unlike apprenticeships in other fields, tattooing apprenticeships are usually unpaid and the apprentice is expected to either pay to learn the practice or work in the shop in exchange for learning. Before approaching a tattoo artist to ask to work as an apprentice, there are many things you can do to get ready:

Tattoo artists help clients express themselves by modifying their bodies.
Kristina Kokhanova/iStock/Getty Images

- Learn to draw.
- Practice drawing on flat and curved objects. (Try drawing on fruit or on your hands or your friends.)
- Try using a weighted pencil to simulate the feel of a tattoo machine.
- Look at the work of the best tattoo artists online, in tattoo magazines, and in real life. What can you take away from their work that would make your own work better?

My favorite part is when we're done and people look at it—the expression on their face. It's so different every time. They could be standing there crying because I did a portrait of their child. Or it makes them feel like they're wearing armor—that nothing can hurt them now. They modify themselves—change who they are. It's very humbling.
—Manuel Vega, tattoo artist

- Take photos of your best drawings to make a portfolio to show the tattoo artist.
- Look up the laws and licensing regulations for tattoo artists and tattoo parlors in your state—you'll be ahead before you begin.

Like other craft artists, you probably won't get rich as a tattoo artist, but you can earn a living once you are experienced. On average, tattoo artists earn somewhere between $14,000 and $49,000 a year.[4] That's a pretty big range because it includes people at different stages of their careers. If you work in someone else's shop, you can expect to pay them 60 to 70 percent of what you charge as their commission. If you have a top reputation, your own shop in a great location, and significant experience, you can earn between $60,000 and $80,000 a year.[5] As tattoos have become more socially acceptable across all sectors of society, jobs for tattoo artists have increased as well.

JEWELER

Jewelers are craft artists who make jewelry. Jewelry makers use a wide range of materials to make wearable art pieces. Jewelry can be made from gold, silver, other metals, wood, glass, precious and semiprecious stones, beads, plastic, and any other material the jewelry designer wants to use.

Good jewelry design is also all about technique. . . . Technique provides designers with the knack to create designs on paper or with a CAD (Computer-Aided Design) program; it is the ability of a jewelry designer to know if a red garnet will stand out against a gold pendant. Technique determines if a piece is wearable or durable. If it is too long, too short, or is too difficult to get on and off. Jewelry designers must know how to manipulate their designs, how to make alterations based on customer feedback. Technique allows the creation of beautiful pieces by using a saw, clay, a torch, hammer, nails, a kiln, and other tools that take ideas from conception to completion, and helps jewelry come to life.—The Art Career Project[6]

A hand-crafted piece of jewelry is an aesthetic expression for the person who makes it and the person who wears it. *South_agency/E+/Getty Images*

According to the BLS, "Jewelers and precious stone and metal workers design, construct, adjust, repair, appraise and sell jewelry."[7] The BLS gives the average salary as $39,440 per year. This actually covers a wide range, because there are so many different kinds of jewelers (see the sidebar "Jeweler Jobs").

A successful jewelry artist needs to have artistic talent, dexterity, great hand-eye coordination, and attention to detail. As a craft artist who makes jewelry, you'll need to learn the techniques of jewelry making. You can learn jewelry-making techniques by taking classes, watching videos, or working with other jewelers who have the skills you want to learn. Jewelry design is taught at every level, from certificates, to associate's degrees, to bachelor's degree, even master's degrees.

Craft artist jewelry designers and makers typically work in their own studio or workshop, often in their homes. They sell their work to the public directly at craft fairs and festivals as well as online, and through boutiques, jewelry

JEWELER JOBS

The US Bureau of Labor Statistics defines different types of jewelers in these categories:

- *Bench jewelers*, also known as metalsmiths, silversmiths, goldsmiths, and platinumsmiths, are the most common type of jewelers. They possess a wide array of skills. They usually do tasks ranging from simple jewelry cleaning and repair to making molds and pieces from scratch. Some specialize in particular tasks such as repairs, hand engraving, stringing, wax carving/model making, enameling, stone cutting, soldering, stone setting, and hand building.
- *Gemologists* analyze, describe, and certify the quality and characteristics of gemstones. After using microscopes, computerized tools, and other grading instruments to examine gemstones or finished pieces of jewelry, they write reports certifying that the items are of a particular quality. Most gemologists have completed the Graduate Gemologist program through the Gemological Institute of America.
- *Jewelry appraisers* carefully examine jewelry to determine its value and then write appraisal documents. They determine value by researching the jewelry market and by using reference books, auction catalogs, price lists, and the internet. They may work for jewelry stores, appraisal firms, auction houses, pawnbrokers, or insurance companies. Many gemologists also become appraisers.
- *Jewelry designers* create design concepts and manage the prototype and modelmaking process.
- *Production jewelers* fabricate and assemble pieces in a manufacturing setting and typically work on one aspect of the manufacturing process.[8]

stores, museum shops, or other retail outlets. Some craft jewelers teach jewelry-making classes and workshops, and give demonstrations for the public.

Craft jewelers may also work as bench jewelers for a jewelry company or store, or as production jewelers for a jewelry company. They may also develop their own named line of jewelry that is sold through a larger jewelry company.

> I know people who are really talented in their craft but don't have people skills and marketing skills, so they don't do well. It's not that they don't make good things. You need to learn marketing skills. Marketing is just as important as how good a craftsperson you are. You have to believe in yourself, and not be shy, and be able to take criticism. You have to know what you have and what you can offer. You have to be able to speak up and talk to people. You can believe in it, but you have to express it. Get to know your customers, be interested in them as well, I like that approach, just having a personal interest in people.—Tom Kuhner, jeweler

THOMAS KUHNER—JEWELER

Thomas Kuhner (center).
Courtesy of Hadrian Hatfield

Tom Kuhner is the owner of Thomas Kuhner Hand Wrought Jewelry in Sanbornton, New Hampshire. After earning a bachelor's degree in mass communication from the Ohio State University, he decided to learn to make jewelry. He works with gold and silver using traditional metalsmithing methods, and includes precious and semiprecious stones and freshwater pearls. His work can be seen in shops, galleries, and juried craft fairs around the country, as well as on his website at www.thomaskuhner.com. People interested in talking with Tom about the life and career of a jeweler can contact him at thomaskuhner@gmail.com.

How did you become interested in making jewelry?

My father was a dentist, he did his own lab work, and he would sometime make jewelry in his lab. He would make a wax model and cast it from gold, because he had the materials. That was my earliest memory of something that impressed me. After college, I needed to find something to do in my life, and I didn't know what it was. I met a jeweler in Rockport, Massachusetts, who employed people to make jewelry. That appealed to me. There was a long waiting list, but I'd write him letters and inquire. About a year passed, an opening came up and, because I'd kept in touch, they offered it to me. I worked for him for six years. He always encouraged us to make jewelry on our own. I established some wholesale accounts and did some retail fairs. Then I decided I'd try the Buyers Market for American Crafts. (The other main trade show is the American Craft Council.) I applied and got accepted in the winter of 1979–1980. That year, the prices of silver and gold went up dramatically, and I was laid off. It turned out to be a blessing. It was different working on my own. I liked the variety of what I had to do, going to shows, taking orders, doing everything myself. I just slowly enlarged the shows that I did, and I continued to go back to the wholesale show for many years. It's a lot of work, but it always turns out pretty well. I did wholesale and retail for many years. I got big enough to hire help to get ready for shows, packaging, finish work. It went on for forty years! I'm on the verge of retiring, but I keep doing one more year and one more year.

What is a typical day on your job?

I always had my shop in my house, so I didn't have a long commute. Our hours were 9 to 5 with an hour off for lunch. I'd look at the mail, see what orders had come in, apply to shows, keep the books. I would usually spend a good amount of time—all day or a half a day—making jewelry. You wear many hats as a small business owner. I enjoyed all of it. I liked having my business at home—you can deduct parts of your house and utilities, car expenses. I had a good accountant who did my taxes and balanced my checkbook. I like being independent and being my own boss. There's more forgiveness in the day, if I felt like taking a break. It was perfect for me. Some people need to work for someone else but for me it was perfect.

What's the best part of your job?

Doing shows and having relationships with customers coming to the booth. Getting to know people, and what they liked and didn't like. Fulfilling their need to find a gift or something for themselves. Their appreciation for what they got. That was satisfying—very rewarding. And having successful shows where we made more than we expected and could go back again the next year.

What's the most challenging part of your job?

For me, coming up with new designs every year. Sometimes it would be put off and put off because we were busy. And I'd have to just come up with something. Usually, I would develop designs early in the year, take them to shows, and see what sold. Sometimes things that I didn't like that much would turn out to be a winner. The complexity of just creating on demand was difficult, then testing them so we could refer them to our wholesale customers as pieces that had been tested in the marketplace. By testing designs, I could offer a guarantee—you can try our work risk free and return it if it doesn't work after thirty days or ninety days. Ninety-nine percent of the time everything would be fine, and I'd have a new customer.

What's the most surprising thing about your job?

For me, I was always grateful that I had a job that really suits me. Some years were very, very good—beyond expectation. One year really surprised me, because every show we did was amazing. Sometimes, it was a surprise to get into a show that I didn't expect to.

Did your education prepare you for the job?

My education for jewelry making was all on the job. A lot of what I learned wasn't taught in school. After that, using common sense in just doing what intuitively was good, that includes how much money to spend—I never took out a loan for my business—I only would spend money I had. I never had credit card debt I couldn't pay the next month. I would live within my means. The business grew every year. I was grateful that every year seemed to be better than the next—there were some ups and downs. I would recommend that to anyone in life in general, but especially in this kind of work. Use good judgment and don't get in over your head.

Is the job what you expected?

I never had expectations! I just thought it was a good fit, and I enjoyed doing what I did. I was grateful for all that. It's a wonderful work environment—being outside at craft shows, having my work at home, having someone working with me.

Where do you see the field going from here?

There's still a place for it. I spend a fair amount of time in Asheville, North Carolina, where there's support and interest in craftsmanship. You have to find your market. There's still a place for handmade American crafts, but it might be more difficult than in the old days. The other thing is finding shows that work for you—publications, word of mouth, asking craftsman who make other things. You can usually tell when you're setting up just from the energy whether it's going to be a success or not.

How can a young person prepare for this career while in high school?

Start young but be open to change. You might start in painting or some art form. Try everything you can and see what pleases you and where your talents lie. Now you can go to school and learn all about crafts. You might learn more at a crafts school than at a college. There are several that offer a whole lot in every craft. Or find a job with someone who will train you as an apprentice, and hopefully pay you, and go from there. Or do both—do the craft education thing and then work for someone else for a while. At the craft schools, you can try all the different things you might want to do and the different ways of doing it. You have all these different people who are successes in their business life and can teach you from their experience. There's a lot available—you just have to dig for it.

What is your advice for a young person considering this career?

Go to see some shows and talk to the people. See what their path was. See what schools they recommend. If you're lucky, you could have a good art department in your high school. I know painters and artists that do wonderful work and can support themselves. I know people who are really talented in their craft but don't have people skills and marketing skills, so they don't do well. It's not that they don't make good things. You need to learn marketing skills. Marketing is just as important as how good a craftsperson you are. You have to believe in yourself, and not be shy, and be able to take criticism. You have to know what you have and what you can offer. You have to be able to speak up and talk to people. You can believe in it, but you have to express it. Get to know your customer, be interested in them as well, I like that approach, just having a personal interest in people.

How Are Job Prospects for Craft Artists?

Craft artists of all kinds sell their work to customers and collectors and work on commission to create pieces that a specific client is looking for. Many craft artists supplement their income with other jobs—such as teaching art or working in production or in an industry related to their craft.

Most craft artists are self-employed entrepreneurs, so to a certain extent, your "job prospects" are what you make them. Your net income will depend on things like the kind of work you make, what materials you use, how long it takes to make a piece, how well-known you are, and how much work you sell in a year. We'll go into this in more detail in chapter 4.

In the next chapter, learn how to form a craft artist career plan.

Forming a Career Plan

A career as a craft artist brings your creativity together with customers who want your unique products. *kali9/E+/Getty Images*

Preparing for a Craft Artist Career

There are many different roads that lead to craft artist careers. You might show and sell your work in galleries or museum stores in major cities like New York or London. You might travel the country, selling your crafts directly to the public from your own booth at outdoor art fairs and festivals. You might create work on commission, working with clients to develop a design that meets their needs and represents you as a craft artist. You may also have another job to support yourself while you build or carry out your craft art career. (See the following section, "If You're Good at Craft Arts, You Can Also . . .")

As a craft artist, you make things that people can use and that enhance their lives. When someone buys your piece and takes it home, your self-expression can become their self-expression. This difference between making crafts for your own enjoyment and making them as a professional is the willingness to keep getting better, to work with people to help them express themselves through your craft work, to work long, hard hours, and to keep track of the business side of things as well as the artistic side.

A small part of me looked at this like it was a job, but it's not—it's a lifestyle. From my journeys all over the world, I've learned there are different kinds of tattooers. If you strive to be one of the best—not just at tattooing but everything—then it's a lifestyle. You're a tattoo artist, not just a tattooer.—Manny Vega, tattoo artist

Building Skills

Of course, the first thing you need to do to prepare for a career as a craft artist is to learn and perfect your craft. You can start right now by making things, taking classes or workshops, and asking for feedback from experts on how to make what you make better and better. Chapter 3 goes into detail about the paths of education and apprenticeship that craft artists follow to reach mastery in their fields.

When you read the interviews with craft artists in this book, you'll see that despite doing very different kinds of crafts and coming from very different backgrounds, they all have certain things in common: a desire to keep learning and to keep developing their skills. Even as professionals, they know they are never finished learning and that there is always some way to improve their skills, their creative vision, and their final products.

I want to keep improving my skills to bring the creative ideas I have to life and to form. That's a big part of being a craftsperson—you have to get your skills to the point where you can realize your ideas. I have a lot to learn, and I look forward to learning it.—Liz Grace, woodworker

Building Relationships

Being a successful professional craft artist begins with making beautiful, well-crafted pieces, but there's more to it. You'll need to build personal relationships and interact with the public effectively. What does that mean? Well, the main thing is to treat other people the way you'd want to be treated. Other people are just people—like you—with their own points of view and their own priorities that are just as important to them as yours are to you. Take pride in your talent and skills, but don't be arrogant about them. Be respectful and friendly to everyone. You can learn something new and important from almost everyone you meet.

Teachers and Mentors

Your teachers include anyone you learn from. Of course, you have teachers at school, in college, or at a craft school. But you could also learn from someone you know who can show you how to use equipment or follow a plan, or from a master craftsperson who takes you on as an apprentice.

When you begin learning your craft, it's important to remember that learning craft arts is based on "tradition, honor, and respect" (in the words of tattoo artist Manuel Vega). When a professional craft artist shares their knowledge and skills with you, they are helping you because they want to—not because they have to. Even when you are paying for a class or a workshop, remember to treat your teachers with respect. Listen to what they say and honor the fact that they are willing to share their hard-earned knowledge with you.

Craft Community

Craft artists agree that it's important to be part of the community of artists who practice your craft. Your community is a deep source of knowledge about the skills and techniques of making what you make, as well as useful experience in how to run a craft business. But the most important thing about being part of your craft community is the opportunity to hang with people who like what you like and do what you do (or hope to do).

Craft artists are, on the whole, welcoming and generous people who are happy to help you. Be sure to repay that kindness by accepting help with gratitude and respect, and by "paying it forward" to those who come to you for help and advice in the future.

Stockists

The galleries and shops that stock your work on a regular basis to sell to their retail customers are your stockists. This is an important, ongoing relationship. Many of these outlets may be far away from where you live, so you'll be dealing with them by phone and e-mail. It's very important to be both professional and easy to work with in order to build these long-term relationships. We'll talk more about stockists below in the section "Selling Your Work."

Customers

With luck, you'll be interacting with customers all the time—at craft fairs, trunk shows, open studios, in your own shop, or working on commission. It's important to be friendly and welcoming as well as professional when dealing with customers. When customers like and respect you as a person as well as an artisan, they are more likely to become repeat customers and to recommend you and your work to their friends.

Selling Your Work

As a craft artist, you'll be out in the world making connections with people who might buy, stock, or commission your work. You'll also meet people who might not buy something right away, but will remember you when they think about owning a piece of craft art or recommending a craft artist to a friend. If they have a positive experience with you, they'll want to come back!

Your Place

Being able to welcome customers to your own shop, studio, or workshop is one of the best ways to connect with customers. People are curious about what you do—how you make the cool, unique things you make—and like to be able to picture you in your work environment. It makes them feel like they are part of the creative action. And it puts your work at a natural advantage, with no competing pieces by other artisans and a roomful of work that already "works and plays well together."

If you plan to run a shop or store where you can welcome people to purchase what you make, there are a few things you'll need to know about. A course in small-business management is probably a good idea. While we can't go into all the details of running a retail store here, you'll need to be aware of:

- The business licenses and permits required by local and state governments
- Fire and other safety codes and requirements
- Whether you will need any employees and what employment rules apply
- What hours you'll be open—these will need to be consistent, as people get frustrated by shops that are closed when they're supposed to be open

If you don't want to run a store but would like to welcome visitors to your studio, host occasional open-studio events, instead. You can set up your own open-studio event or tie it in with local or regional open studios.

QUICK TIPS FOR AN OPEN-STUDIO EVENT

Think of an open studio as a party you're hosting for people who are or might be interested in what you make. Not a wild party—a nice party.

If you're part of a community open-studio event or art crawl, be sure to get in touch with the organizers well in advance to be sure that you and your space are included on the map and in all the publicity. But don't stop there!

Whether you're part of a group or hosting your own open studio, you'll need to take care of some things, like:

BEFORE

- Have an up-to-date and complete mailing list.
- E-mail and/or postcard mailing with great images of the best available work and clear information about who, what, when, where, and parking.
- Send out a press release announcing the open studio, with all the relevant details about who, what, when, where, and parking.
- Clean! Be sure your space is as clean as you can make it for visitors, especially the bathroom.
- Display! Set up displays of your work. Include a "display" of work in progress, tools, etc.
- Purchase refreshments and serving items (plates, cups, napkins)—you don't have to go overboard, but it's a nice way to welcome people to your open studio.

DURING

- Be on time and dressed nicely—your own clothes but not your dirty, work clothes
- Have someone there to help you and keep you company while you're waiting for people to show up (this person can also make sure people have refreshments, that trash gets disposed of, and can talk to visitors while you're talking to other visitors)
- Have a way for people to pay if they want to buy something (like a credit card reader you can put on your phone)
- Have a way to remember who came—have them sign the guestbook and include their e-mail. Some open studios include a jar to drop in business

cards (or slips of paper with the same information) for a later drawing to win a small piece or reproduction.

- Welcome the people who come in and be prepared to talk to them about what you make, how you make it, and what you like most about it.
- Be yourself or better—if you're negative, pessimistic, or sullen, people will want to avoid you and your work. Do your work a favor and be your best self. Be positive and answer questions. Treat everyone well, even if their questions seem ignorant.
- Don't be surprised if you don't sell anything—most visitors will just be curious, but some might want to buy something at another time.
- Give them something to take away—this could be a postcard, brochure, or magnet with a great image of your work, your website, and your contact information.
- Thank them for coming.

AFTER

- Track how many visitors came and add any new people to your mailing list.
- Send out an e-mail message thanking people for coming.
- Follow up on any leads for purchases or commissions.
- Get back to work!

Fairs and Festivals

Rows of tents filled with colorful craft arts surrounded by eager visitors is the scene most people think of first when they hear that you are a craft artist. This is a great way to meet and interact with customers, find out what kind of work resonates with people most, and see what other craft artists are doing.

Before you decide to try for a vendor booth at a craft fair, be sure you know something about the fair. Attend a few shows, walk around, and look at the quality of crafts that are available. Be sure your work is ready to compete. Ask other craftspeople which shows they think are the best. And don't just talk to people who do what you do! If you're a potter, go ahead and ask a glass artist or a jeweler or a dollmaker which shows they like best.

Customers look forward to meeting craft artists and buying their products at fairs, festivals, and bazaars. *JackF/iStock/Getty Images*

GETTING IN

When you're first starting out, it's a good idea to get your feet wet at a craft fair that's open to anyone who pays for a space. It's a great way to practice and get an idea of all the expected and unexpected details that come up when you're a vendor. These fairs usually advertise for vendors three to six months ahead of time. In some cases, you can get in at the last minute if there is space available.

Larger fairs are often juried and your work has to be accepted before you can sign up. Be sure to submit excellent photos of your best work and follow submission instructions *exactly*.

Whether juried or open, you will need to be sure you get all the important information from the people in charge of the fair:

- Booth size—are there different sizes available?
- What are the booth costs?
- Are tents and/or movable walls available?
- Is electricity available?
- Is lighting available? If not, can you bring your own?

- Do they provide tables and chairs or should you bring your own?
- What time do they open for setup?
- Where should you park? Can you drive up to your booth area? If so, can you park there or do you have to return your car to the parking lot before visitors arrive?
- What time do the gates open for visitors? What time do they close?
- Where will your booth be (near food? near bathrooms? near the main thoroughfare?)
- What rules and regulations do they want you to follow?

Other things you'll need to factor in are your travel and shipping expenses (for you *and* your friend). It's important to know how much you need to sell to break even. If you don't think you'll break even, try for a smaller show closer to home.

GETTING READY

Have enough items to sell. Some people may want to order larger items to be delivered, or get in touch about a commission, but most visitors will want to buy something they can take with them. You don't want to run out!

Plan your pricing. If you have specific prices already set, you can make up a price list and prep your tags ahead of time. Some vendors recommend waiting to price until you're at the fair, so you can stay in the same range as other craft artists in your medium.

Be sure to bring everything you will need. Make a checklist so nothing gets behind. For instance (in alphabetical order), you'll want to be sure to pack:

- Bags and tissue paper for sold items—paper bags with handles make the best impression
- Business cards (with your website and Instagram on them)
- Business card holder (so they don't blow away)
- Cashbox and $20 to $50 in small bills for change (for cash sales)—be sure it locks and that you have the key to open it again
- Chairs—a couple of stools or folding chairs
- Credit card reader
- Photobook of your other work (with detailed shots!) for visitors to look through

- Price tags or stickers and a pen (in fact, bring several pens—you never know when one will dry up)
- Receipt book—a great way to collect customer information so you can add them to your mailing list
- Shelves—if you can transport shelves to the fair, it will give you more room to display your work and add vertical interest to your display area
- Sign with your business name, website, and some photos
- Specialized display racks, mirror, props to enhance your display
- Table—a lightweight folding table is not very expensive, but stacked boxes will work if you don't have access to a table
- Tablecloths—nothing fancy; twin-size white bedsheets work fine
- Tent (unless one is provided)—be sure you know how to set it up and take it down easily

Bring a friend! You could share a booth with another craft artist or just bring along a friend who likes craft fairs. Everything is easier if you have someone to help you haul your stuff from the car, set it all up, make food runs, and hold down the fort when you need to go to the bathroom.

SETTING UP

- If you followed your checklist, you'll have everything you need to set up. Be sure to create an attractive display. If you can make some work while you're there, visitors will come to watch.
- Set up your table in front, with your business cards and your sign.
- Arrange your goods on the table and the shelves. Be sure everything is priced.
- Keep your folding chairs handy but don't sit in them when there are customers around. You look more welcoming when you're standing up. The exception is if you are actually making something—then sit down if you usually work sitting.
- Take the time to meet the other vendors (especially the ones closest to your booth) and walk around to see where things are and what kind of crafts are being offered.
- Before the gates open to the public, be sure you eat something and go to the bathroom.

SELLING YOUR WARES

- Greet visitors, answer questions, smile, but don't push for sales.
- Be pleasant and professional, with a little added warmth.
- Make it easy to buy—know how to use your credit card reader and take cash gracefully and quickly.
- Provide receipts and record customer contact information (especially e-mail addresses) on your copy.
- Wrap purchases carefully (especially breakables) in tissue before putting them in bags.
- Have your friend take photos of you in your booth—smile!

FOLLOWING UP

- Figure out how much money you took in and then subtract your expenses. Did you make a profit? Or at least break even? That helps you know if you should do that particular fair again. In any case, fairs should only be one revenue stream for a craft artist.
- Did you build your mailing list? Add the names and e-mail addresses to your mailing list, then send out an e-mail announcement with photos saying how well it went.
- Start looking for fairs to do next year!

Trade Shows

Trade shows are where craft artists can show their latest work and take wholesale orders from store buyers, architects, interior designers, and museum catalog buyers. There are numerous trade shows every year—some are specific to particular crafts and some are open to all kinds of work.

Before signing up for a trade show, it's important to know which trade show is right for you and what you make. A good place to start is with *Handmade Business* magazine (formerly *The Crafts Report*), which lists many trade shows on its website along with information on what kind of show it is, expected attendance, booth fees, and contact information.[1]

Trade shows let buyers get to know your craft arts and place orders.
Giselleflissak/E+/Getty Images

As with a fair, be sure you know what all your costs will be (entry fee, booth fee, travel and expenses, what you can bring and what costs extra to have at your booth). It's a more intense environment than a craft fair, so you'll need stamina and helpers.

If you want to sell your craft art on a wholesale basis, you should be ready to produce a large amount of inventory and be able to respond quickly to fulfill orders on time. Will you have to hire help? What will the additional shipping and delivery costs be like?

Trunk Shows

A trunk show is a partnership between a retailer and a craft artist. You bring a certain number of pieces or samples to the store, and the store invites its customers to come and purchase them either through the store or directly from you. You make sales and the store can see which items are most popular so it can stock these on a more regular basis.

Trunk shows make customers feel like they are part of something special. These can be held in almost any type of retail outlet, but are most popular in small boutiques and speciality stores, as well as bridal outlets.

In her posts for Fashion Brain Academy, marketing expert Jane Hamill has some great advice for booking and putting on a trunk show.[2] Here's the quick version:

- Ask if the shop has displays you can use or if you need to bring your own.
- Find out how and where your items will be displayed.
- Ask how much to bring, what the store's markup is, and how the items should be ticketed.
- If you sell wearable craft art, see if the shop team can be wearing your wares during the trunk sale.
- Promote! Find out what promotion the store will be doing and coordinate with them about the additional promotion you'll be doing.
- Show up early on the day and get set up.
- Look the part—wear your own designs if they're wearable; otherwise, dress like the creative person you are.
- Have your own order/receipt book to help you maintain your records of who buys what and who should be added to your mailing list. This not only backs up the store's records but can include specifics and special instructions that will make more sense to you than to them.
- Make sure your wares are displayed well, and include some nice tabletop signs, tablecloths, maybe flowers—sometimes the store's idea of a good job will be different from yours. For the day of the trunk sale, make sure your work is shown to its best advantage.
- It's okay to leave some items on consignment with the store after the show if you are comfortable with the arrangement and trust the people.
- After the show, follow through on your orders and your promises. Don't lose your momentum! This is the part that makes people want to do business with you again.
- Stay in touch with the store and the customers you met there. People like to buy from people they know.
- Overdeliver by including nice packaging and a handwritten note in any shipped orders.

- Remember that you are not just selling the piece of craft art—you are selling the story. Tell your story to the people who come to the trunk show, and have a nice printed piece with information about you, what you make, and what compels you to make it that they can take away with them.

Trunk shows are a good way to get to know the retailers who could become your . . .

Stockists

The term "stockist" is used to mean any retail establishment—store, boutique, gallery, whatever—that stocks your work to sell to its customers. This is (ideally) a long-term relationship where you supply a certain number of pieces at an agreed-upon wholesale price, the stockist adds their markup, and the customer buys the piece at the final price. For instance, a jeweler might look for boutiques, a glass artist might look for a home goods store, while a blacksmith might look for a gardening or fireplace supply store.

The first step to find the right stockists is to visit shops and galleries to see who sells craft pieces that are compatible with yours and that meets your requirements for a stockist. For instance, you don't want a store that sells things by other craft artists that look too much like yours—you want your pieces to stand out. Start in your local community and work your way out. Look online, as well.

Do some research before you approach a particular stockist or wholesaler:

- Who are their customers?
- What kinds of products do they carry (including price point and quality)?
- How do they promote and market their store?
- How long have they been in business?
- What are their online rankings and customer comments like?
- What do other craft artists think of them? (For instance, do they have a reputation for paying on time?)
- Do they acquire the majority of their stock through wholesale purchase or consignment?

It's worth a little time to do your due diligence and make sure that you are dealing with reputable stockists whose customers are most likely to appreciate your craft work.

CONSIGNMENT VS. WHOLESALE

What's the difference between placing your work with a stockist through consignment versus wholesale? And does it matter? Yes, it does!

CONSIGNMENT AGREEMENT

When you consign your work to a stockist, you're basically leaving it in their care with the hope that it will sell. The work still belongs to you. You sign a consignment agreement that says what pieces you're leaving, the retail price, your percentage, and their percentage for each piece. It should also define when payment will be made for any pieces that are sold. If the work sells, you get your agreed-on percentage and they get theirs. If the work doesn't sell, you pick it up at the end of the consignment period.

Some stockists, especially art galleries or small boutiques, only work with craft artists on a consignment basis. When listing pieces with a stockist on consignment, it's very important to have everything spelled out in the contract, including who is responsible for the value of the work if there is a fire, break-in, or other disaster, or if they suddenly go out of business.

Be sure you only consign work to people you know and trust, or those who have a terrific reputation among other artisans who sell with them.

WHOLESALE PURCHASE

When a stockist buys work directly from you at your wholesale price (your percentage of the full retail price—usually about 50 percent), they own the piece and it's up to them to sell it in order to make good on that investment. Your job is to deliver the quantity of pieces they need, on time, and in good condition. If your pieces sell well to their customers, they'll order more.

If a stockist gets the majority of their inventory as wholesale purchases, they should purchase your work the same way. Be sure that you are professional and hold up your end of the contract to deliver the amount of work ordered in a timely manner. That will help ensure repeat business.

Working with a client on a commissioned work can be difficult but very rewarding.
Caiaimage/Agnieszka Olek/Caiaimage/Getty Images

Commissions

When someone comes to you and says they want you to make something just for them—that's a commission. Working with a client on a commissioned piece is very different from selling your work in a retail setting. A commission is collaboration with the client, who may have a very specific idea of what they want or may want to leave most of the creative work up to you.

Tips for Commission Success

IN ADVANCE

Know what you can do. What works and what doesn't for you? Think about your style, your subject matter, and how long it takes to complete different types and sizes of pieces. Be able to set a reasonable deadline for yourself.

Know your prices. What do your pieces costs, bearing in mind the time and materials required to make them? Be able to set a reasonable price for your work so you won't be asked to renegotiate.

Have marketing materials ready. Your business card, a high-quality brochure, etc., can be useful both when you first meet a client and when you deliver a commissioned piece.

WORKING WITH THE CLIENT

Communication. Good communication between you and your client *at every stage of the process* is essential. This is what makes the difference between a commission that's successful and one that just isn't.

- Understand what the client wants before you begin.
- Ask for a clear reference image if they can provide one.
- Draft several options and work with the client to finalize a design before you make anything.
- If a problem comes up that will change anything you've agreed on, be sure to communicate with the client immediately.

Contract. Don't start work on a commission without a clear contract that specifies the scope of work and each party's responsibilities, such as (but not limited to):

- What kind of piece will you make? This would include size and materials.
- Who the decision maker is—only deal with one person. If a couple or business wants to commission a piece, be sure the contract names a single person to make final decisions.
- Nonrefundable deposit—the percentage the client must pay you before you begin work. If they cancel the commission for any reason, you should be able to keep the deposit.

I'm working with the customer one-to-one to try to realize their dream with my creativity.—Liz Grace, woodworker

---

- Number of drafts—it's possible to go on designing forever with some customers. Specify the number of design drafts you will do before you begin. There should be no "draft" versions of the actual piece.
- Deadline—when do you need to deliver the final piece?

Behave professionally. Always be polite, professional, reasonable, and friendly. This goes a long way toward establishing a good relationship with your client. You'll need that if you need to make changes to the contract or agreement. Also, a good relationship with clients brings repeat business and good word-of-mouth (i.e., recommendations).

Be treated professionally. If your client can't also manage to be polite, professional, reasonable, and friendly, you might not want to work with them. It's better to let a commission go than to work with someone who is nothing but trouble.

> *Don't be afraid to turn down a commission if something feels off.* If you are not going to be a great fit for this patron, there are plenty of other artists out there who may. Don't feel obligated to accept just because someone asks. Value your own time and skill, and feel free to be selective.—John Middick, *Sharpened Artist*[3]

If You're Good at Craft Arts, You Can Also . . .

There are many jobs that you can do with your craft skills. While you are building your craft business, you may need to support yourself with an additional job. Or you might want to have a related career with regular hours and benefits, while you pursue your craft arts as a "side hustle." Here is a small sampling of the kinds of jobs craft artists hold:

- *Teacher:* Whether you have a regular job teaching arts and crafts at a school or college, or you teach occasional workshops or classes, artisans have specialized skills that only they can teach. Teaching gives you a chance to share what you know while earning some additional income to support your craft art practice.

- *Instructional assistant:* In this role, you would support the teacher by inventorying and maintaining equipment, working one-to-one with students, and supervising student workers.
- *Studio assistant:* Like an apprenticeship, working for a master craftsperson as a studio assistant gives you a chance to learn the business and develop your own skills while you also earn a living. As a studio assistant, you help your boss with all the background support stuff that goes into her or his crafts practice. This can include administrative work, production work, and general back up for fairs, trunks shows, commissions, etc.
- *Studio manager:* Art schools and universities with large art departments sometimes hire studio managers to make sure the studio facilities and classrooms are in good repair, well-equipped, safe, and secure. You'll need to understand the technologies used in the studio as well as safety standards and regulations for these specialized areas.
- *Studio technician:* Art schools and community makerspaces need staff to help students and community members use the equipment safely. People with woodworking and/or metalworking skills are in demand for these jobs. You'll need to have good technical skills, be detail-oriented, alert, and be able to work with people.
- *Glass industry:* Jobs in the glass industry include production of household items, optical products, specialized industrial and medical devices, and more. Some of these jobs require advanced education, such as an engineering degree. Others require only a high school diploma or GED and some hands-on experience.
- *Ceramic industry:* Jobs in the ceramics industry range from entry-level jobs to advanced engineering positions. Depending on the business, you could be making dishes, lamps, tiles, pipes, or other household items or industrial or building materials. People are also needed to schedule and organize production.
- *Metalworking:* People with metalworking skills are in demand as welders, machinists, manufacturing and production workers, as well as industrial blacksmiths who make specialized tools, machine parts, chains, and things like fire escapes and security grills.
- *Traditional crafts demonstration:* History museums and living history sites such as Colonial Williamsburg (Williamsburg, Virginia), Historic

Cold Spring Village (Cape May, New Jersey), and Old Sturbridge Village (Sturbridge, Massachusetts) and even some amusement parks like Dollywood (Pigeon Forge, Tennessee) hire craftspeople skilled in traditional craft arts like woodworking, blacksmithing, glassblowing, ceramics, and more to show how these crafts were practiced in earlier times. In this role, visitors watch you at work while you make craft products for them to buy. Sometimes you might do a hands-on workshop. You'll need to be able to talk while you work, so that visitors feel engaged and learn something.

MANUEL VEGA—TATTOO ARTIST

Manny Vega. *Courtesy of Manny Vega*

Manny Vega is the owner of Custom Tattoo Company, one of the top tattoo parlors in Albuquerque, New Mexico. During his twenty-six years in business, Vega has won more than one hundred awards. He is one of the founders of the New Mexico Coalition of Professional Tattoo and Body Piercers and helped the state of New Mexico develop its standards and practices for tattooing. His work can be seen online at www.customtattoo-nm.com.

How did you become interested in tattooing?

I was born in Oahu and being around Polynesian style *tebori* tattooing, I got to see it growing up and it interested me. I got my first tattoo at twelve. The whole thought process—it's forever. It touched me in a lot of different ways.

How did you learn tattooing?

Back in the '80s and '90s, tattooing wasn't what it is now. Now it's in the limelight. Back then, we were a rare breed—a hidden society. The only way to learn was to get an apprenticeship and have a tattooist teach you everything they knew. I couldn't get an apprenticeship, so I started reading, looking at tattoos, drawing. I would go to a local tattoo shop and look through the window, I would sneak in and get thrown out. I would show the owner my drawings and he'd say they sucked, and I would work to get better to impress him. I would practice on the neighborhood kids. I'm still learning to this day—every day I come in, I still learn something new.

What is a typical day on your job?

I do two appointments a day—1:00 p.m. and 5:00 p.m. At one o'clocks, I get things established or finished. Five o'clocks are longer sessions where I really take a bite out of the tattoo. Evenings, I plan drawings, clean machines, and usually end up around midnight.

What's the best part of your job?

My favorite part is when we're done and people look at it—the expression on their face. It's so different every time. They could be standing there crying because I did a portrait of their child. Or it makes them feel like they're wearing armor—that nothing can hurt them now. They modify themselves—change who they are. It's very humbling.

What's the most challenging part of your job?

Portraits of people! Especially when it's someone who's deceased. When people get a portrait, the last image they have is the one they're bringing to me. If one little thing is off—an eyebrow is too high, the sparkle in their eye, they're going to call you on it. It's emotionally and physically draining to get it perfect every time. Just knowing that you cannot let this person down. You have to take their hands, walk to the gates of hell and back unscathed.

What's the most surprising thing about your job?

The things people tell you in the chair. I never knew tattooing was going to be this therapeutic for people. It's amazing when people will open up and tell you things. I struggle with this—are they telling me because they're in pain or because they trust me this much or because it's part of the process? Any tattooer will tell you that we're part therapist. I've been the first or second person that someone has ever told something to. Sometimes I'm honored they shared that with me and sometimes I'm kind of frightened. You hear things you wish you didn't hear.

Is the job what you expected?

A small part of me looked at this like it was a job, but it's not—it's a lifestyle. From my journeys all over the world, I've learned there are different kinds of tattooers. If you strive to be one of the best—not just at tattooing but everything—then it's a lifestyle. You're a tattoo artist, not just a tattooer.

How do clients find you?

Before the internet and social media, I was known because I was published a lot. I was on the cover of every tattoo magazine on the planet! Now, with Instagram, Facebook, my website—they see a tattoo I did on someone or Google award-winning artists. Back in the day, to get known you had to get published and to get published, you had to win awards.

What's your educational background?

I left school in the eleventh grade when I was sixteen. I never graduated or got a GED. I went on the JD Crow national tattoo tour at sixteen, where I was recognized as one of the youngest professional tattoo artists.

What are the hygiene rules that affect tattoo businesses?

Sterility, cleanliness—it's mostly common sense. Everything we use is disposable, comes presterilized. You need to understand pathogens, the difference between clean, sanitized, and sterilized, what to touch and not touch with dirty gloves. One of the biggest issues I've seen through the years is not so much the equipment but the artist themselves, not keeping themselves clean. There's no difference between a tattoo artist and an artist who works for Disney and shows up for work in a three-piece suit and a briefcase. If the artist doesn't care about themselves, they don't care about you.

Do tattoo artists need to be trained and licensed?

Each state is different. In New Mexico, you have to have a license to tattoo. You have to be apprenticed to a licensed tattoo artist, know how to bandage a tattoo, deal with someone who passes out in the chair, how to handle different crises that arise. You present all that to the board and get your license. I opened in 1993, before tattooing was legal. I couldn't ask for a license to tattoo, so I said I wanted to open a business as a dermagraphic technician. In 1998 or 1999, when we created the NM Coalition of Professional Tattoo and Body Piercers, my studio was a training facility, so whenever they were training a new inspector, they'd bring them to my studio and I'd show them what to look for. About ten years ago, the state took over. We were part of the board of barbers and cosmetologists, and now there's a tattoo board. I'm grandfathered in because I'm one of the guys who created the board!

How can a young person prepare for this career while in high school?

The industry is built on respect. Tradition, honor, and respect are the three keys. The best thing to do is to find the artist you would want to tattoo your whole body. Go to that artist and get tattooed by them. Let them know you're an artist and want to do this. Ask them to look at your portfolio of drawings and paintings. You're working your way into a lifestyle. Apprentices don't get hired or paid. You pay to be an apprentice with a signed contract. Or the traditional way, you come in, sweep, clean toilets, work your way in—probably 99 percent of professional tattoo artists have done it that way. No matter what kind of artist you are, when you come in to learn from someone how to tattoo, you're going to tattoo like them—if they're dirty, you will be too. If their work sucks, your work will. It's like a disease feeding a disease. So find someone who does good work and does it right.

What is your advice for a young person considering this career?

Stay off drugs and alcohol—that's the number one killer. When you're semi-good or good, you can make all the money you need for the month in a week. It's tempting to spend the next three weeks partying. Keep your nose clean. If your work is good, you're desired, you're wanted, you're going to have a lot of people wanting to be around you. Be careful and use common sense. You can make a huge difference in the tattoo world if you keep your head straight and give back to the world of tattooing. For something that gave me a life and a roof over my head and clothes on my back, I do think about what I'm giving back. I'd like to know for a fact that I made it better.

What do you think about being part of a professional/artistic community?

It's definitely important to be part of it, but at the same time, you're not. There are good people and bad people, just as in anything. There are bad people that I don't associate with because they do slimy things. But you meet the good people, the good artists, to stay in the loop, stay up on what's going on in the tattoo world, different techniques, different products, recommendations from people. If you need to go somewhere and tattoo in another place, you have a home. I can go anywhere in the world and have a job for a week. It's really important to stay together. And you have those moments where you sit back and wonder if it's worth it, and you talk to people in the industry that you trust and they refill your tank.

What's next, where do you see yourself going from here?

I see myself right now as on the cusp of another change. I think instead of two people a day, I'd rather do one. I want to really push myself even harder to achieve a certain style and look in my work. It's frustrating to not be there yet—but that's the journey.

Where do you see the field going from here?

There's a handful of us "lifers" left—the younger generation doesn't always have the tradition, honor, and respect value. They all want to be rock stars—be on TV shows. It's up to guys like me to teach this to people.

What is one thing you know now that you wish you'd known about the business of being a tattoo artist when you first started out?

Save money. Professional artists, we don't get sick leave, paid vacation, a retirement fund. Either meet a significant other with a retirement fund or keep tattooing until your body gives out.

========================

Pursuing the Education Path

Learning from and with others is the best way to develop your hands-on skills and deep craft knowledge. *SrdjanPav/E+/Getty Images*

Do Craft Artists Need to Study Their Craft?

Absolutely—craft artists need to study both the art and the craft of their medium. Some craft artists learn through a traditional college program at a two-year or four-year school or a trade school. Some learn by taking courses at a school that is focused on teaching that particular craft (such as the Pilchuck Glass School) or one that focuses on a variety of traditional crafts (such as the Penland School of Crafts). Others work as apprentices and learn from a master of the craft. And others begin a craft as a hobby—learning from local classes, from friends, or from online videos—and then make it their life's work.

For craft artists, learning is a lifelong process. Whether you go to art or craft school or not, as a craft artist you not only must continue learning all your life, *you will want to*. As you pursue your craft, the desire to make your work better and better will prompt you to seek out new ways to learn, new aspects of your craft, new techniques and methods, and new business practices so your craft can be your livelihood but still give you plenty of time to create.

First and foremost, learning your craft means learning by doing—creating, more creating, discarding unsuccessful work and keeping successful work, and then more creating. Learn new techniques or approaches by taking classes. Follow artists you like on social media. Watch YouTube videos to see how different artists approach their work or pick up new techniques that enhance the kind of work you do. Read books on art history and journals on contemporary art. Go to galleries and museums, and get to know other artists, gallerists, arts administrators, and collectors.

Preparing for College

How do your prepare yourself to become a craft artist? Before you begin school, experience as much as you can. Take classes, go to exhibits and craft shows, look at books and magazines related to your craft, scroll through Instagram. Most important, look for organizations near you where you can meet other people who are already professionals in your craft. They have a wealth of information!

While You're Still in High School

Does your school offer courses in the craft you love? If they do—take all the classes you can. If not, take art classes, industrial arts classes, and business classes. Whatever your school offers, take it. Get to know your teachers and ask them for feedback on your work. How can you make it better? Are there any common mistakes you're making that you could fix? Do they notice anything about the work that makes it special? Even if a particular teacher doesn't have good answers for these questions, it's good to get in the mind-set of asking them. Be respectful and polite, consider what you're being told even if it doesn't make

> One thing having a degree does is show that you have the motivation and tenacity to do what you set out to do—to yourself as well as others. You learn how to dig around and find the information you need.—Liz Grace, woodworker

sense to you at the time. It might become clear later on. Also, your high school teachers are the first people you'll want to ask for college recommendations.

In addition to high school art and craft classes—or if you don't have access to these classes in school—seek out community craft classes. These are usually taught by professional craftspeople who know a lot about their own medium. This is an opportunity to take classes that aren't offered at your school, or to go deeper in a medium that speaks to you (glassblowing, ceramics, forging, cooking, etc.)

Many high schools offer classes like:

- Ceramics
- Drawing
- Woodworking
- Metalworking
- Culinary arts

Community crafts classes are often offered by local nonprofit arts centers in afterschool programs and/or summer camps. Sometimes craft professionals will offer classes in their own studios to individual students or small groups. Classes will vary based on which artists are available to teach and what they do, but often include things like:

- Bookbinding
- Ceramics
- Enamels
- Fiber art
- Flower arranging
- Forging
- Glass
- Jewelry making
- Leather work

- Mixed media
- Sewing and fashion
- Stone setting and casting
- Upcycling
- Woodturning
- Woodworking

Take advantage of any opportunity to take a class that's in any kind of way related. Look first for high school trade programs, industrial arts programs, or art programs that teach you how to draw something out. Look for community college programs or craft schools that offer blacksmith programs.—Sue Howerter, blacksmith

SEE CRAFTS IN PERSON

The best way to see crafts of all kinds is in person. So go where they are! If you are lucky enough to have a local art or craft museum or two, go again and again. Look at all the collections and spend some time with your favorite pieces. Go to art fairs and craft festivals—don't miss the demonstrations! If you can travel to a "living history museum" like Colonial Williamsburg in Virginia or Old Sturbridge Village in Massachusetts, you can see master craftsmen demonstrating traditional craft arts using traditional methods.

MAKE, MAKE, MAKE

You do this already, right? So keep it up! Don't limit yourself to class assignments. Make what *you* want to make, too. Keep a sketchbook. It's a great place to plan the pieces you want to make and keep notes on the work that inspires you. Draw a lot!

The work you do prior to applying to college, trade school, or an apprenticeship will make up the portfolio you use to apply. Keep track of all your best pieces and be sure to have excellent digital images of them made.

Look for classes and workshops so you
can make, make, make.
*Highwaystarz-Photography/iStock/
Getty Images*

Finding the Education Path for You

Finding the right educational path will help you get started on the life and career you want to pursue. Will that be college? Community or technical college? Bachelor's degree? Apprenticeship? Or some other path?

Let's look first at college, because with a college degree you'll be in a good position to make your work and run your business, as well as have the knowledge and skills you might need to support yourself while getting your craft business established.

Finding the College for You

It's easy to get swamped by all the information that's out there about how and why to choose a particular school for college. There's so much to consider!

One aspect of choosing a school that you might not have heard so much about is fit. It's hard to describe what "fit" means, but students know it when they feel it. It's the feeling you get when you visit a campus and it sticks out in your mind beyond the others you've been to. When you hear yourself saying, "This is the one!"—you've found your fit.

But what goes into that feeling of fit? The best way to be sure you can find the right place for you is to think about what matters to you and narrow down your choices. Ask yourself these questions and write down the answers so you can refer to them when you're checking out schools online and in person. This list is not in any particular order—make a note, as well, of what you would consider your top three most important factors. Some will be more important to you than others, some might not be important to you at all.

ACCREDITATION

Before applying to any college or university, be sure that it holds the right accreditation. While it might seem like national accreditation is better than regional accreditation, the opposite is actually true. According to the website EDSmart:

> Regional accreditation is older and more prestigious than national, except in a few cases. Most non-profit colleges have regional accreditation, not national accreditation . . . regional accrediting organizations operate in specific regions of the country. These organizations grant accreditation to schools, colleges, and universities showing that their credits and degrees meet minimum standards. This is a voluntary process that self-regulates the higher education industry.
>
> Regionally accredited colleges are mostly academically-oriented, non-profit or state-owned institutions. Regionally accredited institutions are reluctant to accept transfer credits from nationally accredited institutions, mainly because the latter hasn't met the stringent standards of faculty qualifications and library resources.[1]

In addition to institutional accreditation, you should also look for programs that are accredited by their appropriate organization. For instance, the National Association of Schools of Art and Design (NASAD) is the leading accrediting body for art and design programs. This kind of accreditation is not required and some schools don't choose to have their programs accredited, but in general, accreditation gives a "seal of approval" that tells you the program meets certain standards.

SIZE

A school of twenty-five hundred people feels quite different from one with forty thousand people. Each size has its pros and cons. You might prefer the intimacy of a small campus, but find that you don't have enough academic or social options there. You might think you're going to feel lost on a large campus, but find your peers within your department, which might feel like a small school within a big one. It's a good idea to visit schools of different sizes, and tour the department you're interested in as well as the general campus. If you happen to meet a few faculty members or students, so much the better!

In a college art or crafts degree program, you will learn the design, drawing, and other skills that will make you a highly accomplished artisan. *javi_indy/iStock/Getty Images*

LOCATION

There are two primary considerations when you're thinking about the location of your school.

1. *Community:* What kind of place do you want to be? Colleges can be found in small towns, suburbs, small cities, big cities, and in rural areas,

too. Where do you feel most comfortable? You'll be there for several years—is it important to you to be able to go hiking or go out to restaurants and concerts? What about travel? Do you want easy access to an airport or train station? Do you want to be able to go to the beach or visit nearby towns and cities?

2. *Distance from home*: If your program can be found in a community college (sometimes called a junior college), you may not have to go far at all. Many community college students are "commuters"—they live at home or on their own and come to the campus for classes and activities. Often, community college students don't need to live in a dorm. At four-year colleges and universities, it's much more common to live in a dorm. But if you choose a school close to home, you could commute to a four-year school, also. Or do both—live on campus and go home on the weekends.

So how do you feel? Are you ready to strike out on your own and take on the adventure of living far from home? Or do you want to be able to get home easily, do your laundry, and indulge in Dad's apple pie? Sometimes, students who are the first in their family to go to college find that if they live at home, their parents expect them to continue certain responsibilities, like taking care of younger siblings. That can really eat into your study and studio time. Think about your home situation and whether or not there will be a lot of distractions when you think about living on or off campus. Of course, life on campus comes with its own distractions, so you need to remember that, too.

ACADEMIC ENVIRONMENT

Does the school offer the majors or craft programs that you want? Does it have the right level of degree program? What percent of classes are taught by professors and what percent are taught by teaching assistants or adjunct instructors? Does the school offer internships, or help you find internships? Are there study abroad programs associated with your interests? Do they offer everything you want to take, or is it possible to do independent study to fill in the gaps?

FINANCIAL AID OPTIONS

This is something you have to look at carefully—see the "Financial Aid" section below. Does the school provide a lot of scholarships, grants, work-study jobs, or other opportunities? How much does the cost of school play a role in your decision?

SUPPORT SERVICES

Support services include things like academic counseling, career counseling, health and wellness, residence services, the financial aid office, information technology support, commuter services, and services for students who are disabled, or who have families, or who are lesbian, gay, bisexual, or transgender. Some schools also have religious services, such as a chaplain. Before you choose a school, look through the website and be sure it provides the services you will need.

CLUBS/ACTIVITIES/SOCIAL LIFE

Most colleges have clubs and other social activities on campus, whether the student population is mostly residents or mostly commuters. Look for clubs related to the craft you're interested in, as well as clubs and activities that meet your other interests. There may be concerts, plays, poetry readings, art shows, sports, and more on your college campus.

SPECIALIZED PROGRAMS

Does the school or program you're looking at have any programs that meet your specialized needs? For instance, some institutions have programs specifically for veterans. Some address learning disabilities. Do they provide mental health counseling services?

HOUSING OPTIONS

What kind of housing options do you want and need? Does the college provide dorms? How many students will share a room? Are there on-campus apartments? Is there help with finding off-campus housing like apartments or rooms for rent?

TRANSPORTATION

If you live off campus, how will you get to school? Is there a bus system—campus or municipal? Is there a rideshare program? Could you ride a bicycle? Will you need to have access to a car? Is there an on-campus shuttle bus service that can get you around quickly if you're attending a large campus? What will you need to carry from home to school—will your transportation options have room for your stuff?

STUDENT BODY

What's the makeup of the student body? What's the ratio of males to females? Is there enough diversity? Are most of the students residents or commuters? Part time or full time?

Learning from a master artisan. *Geber86/iStock/Getty Images*

Getting In

Some colleges and universities are highly competitive. Others welcome everyone who applies. Some colleges expect students to be enrolled full time and finish a degree program within four or five years. Others are geared toward students who may be taking classes while working full time and raising a family. It's important to know what each school you're considering is like, what they focus on, what kind of work their faculty, students, and graduate students do, and what they're looking for in prospective students.

Go to each school's website and see what they are asking for in your application. If they want examples of specific exercises, be sure to include your best examples in the portfolio you submit to them.

PORTFOLIO

If you're applying to a college or university art department, your portfolio is key. Your portfolio is a showcase of all your *best* work. At different times in your life, it will contain different types or groupings of work, depending on what you're using it for. When you are applying to college, your portfolio should be a broad representation of your best artwork in the various media you use.

WHAT SHOULD YOUR PORTFOLIO CONTAIN?

Different schools will have some different requirements, but in general you want to showcase:

- Ten to twenty examples of your absolute best work (ten great pieces is better than twenty mediocre ones)
- The different media you work in (ceramics? glass? cupcakes?)
- Observational drawings (drawings from life)—include a variety of subject matter, both linear and volume-based work, and remember to also let your own drawing style shine through
- Personal work—pieces that come from your life or experiences in a way that's meaningful to you
- Your most original work—show them your ideas and what you will bring to the experience

- Anything else a specific school has asked you to include, such as your sketchbook

The work in your portfolio should mostly consist of finished pieces: clean, fully realized, framed if that's relevant, and most of all, *well photographed*. The first time a school sees your work may well be in digital images. Be sure your photos do your work justice. Save up or get together with some friends and pool your money to hire a photographer, if you can.

Paying for College

Going to college these days is expensive. Art schools often have very high tuition, plus the cost of housing, food, books, expenses, and art supplies. Schools dedicated to a particular craft may not offer much in the way of financial aid. Community colleges can be much easier on the wallet.

Apply for all the scholarships you can! Scholarship money does not have to be paid back.
Casper1774Studio/iStock/Getty Images

FINANCIAL AID

It is worth your while to put some time and effort into finding out what financial aid you qualify for. Reach out to the financial aid office at the school you want to attend. They can tell you a lot about what you may be able to work out.

Financial aid can come from many sources. The kind of awards you're eligible for depend on a lot of things, such as:

- Merit (the quality of the craft work you've already made)
- Academic performance in high school
- Financial need
- Program/field
- Type of college

NOT ALL FINANCIAL AID IS CREATED EQUAL

Educational institutions tend to define financial aid as any scholarship, grant, loan, or paid employment that assists students to pay their college expenses. Notice that "financial aid" covers both *money you have to pay back* and *money you don't have to pay back*. That's a big difference!

DO NOT HAVE TO BE REPAID

- Scholarships
- Grants
- Work-study

HAVE TO BE REPAID WITH INTEREST

- Federal government loans
- Private loans
- Institutional loans

Scholarships

Scholarships are financial awards that are usually offered on the basis of academic or creative merit. Some scholarships are awarded for other reasons, such as membership in Scouting or some other organization, or for going into a particular field. Scholarships can also be granted to students who have certain characteristics, such as being athletes or female or a member of a minority group. Some scholarships go toward tuition; others are for something specific, like textbooks.

Merit-based scholarships can help offset the cost of your college degree. Scholarships usually pay a portion of tuition—it is very rare to receive a full-tuition scholarship, but it does happen. Scholarships do not have to be paid back. Also, receiving a merit-based scholarship is an important credential to add to your résumé. Scholarships can be local, regional, statewide, or national in scope.

There are also scholarships specifically for community college students, including those who want to transfer to a bachelor's degree program later on or those who are studying a particular subject. Some are offered by professional associations, some by nonprofit organizations, and some by the community colleges themselves.

To learn more about scholarships, check out www.gocollege.com/financial -aid/scholarships/types/.

Grants

Grants are similar to scholarships. Most tuition grants are awarded based on financial need, but some are restricted to students in particular sports, academic fields, demographic groups, or with special talents. Grants do not have to be paid back.

Some grants come through federal or state agencies, such as the Pell Grant, SMART Grants, and Federal Supplemental Education Opportunity Grant (FSEOG). You'll need to fill out the FAFSA form (see below under "Loans"). Learn more about those at https://studentaid.ed.gov/types/grants-scholarships.

Grants can also come from private organizations or from the college itself. For instance, some private colleges or universities have enough financial resources that they can "meet 100 percent of proven financial need." That doesn't mean a free ride, but it usually means some grant money to cover the gap between what the financial aid office believes you can afford and the amount covered by scholarships and federal loans (more on federal loans below).

Work-Study

The federal work-study program provides money for undergraduate and graduate students to earn money through part-time jobs. Work-study is a need-based program, so you'll need to find out if you are eligible for it. Some students are not eligible at first but become eligible later in their college career. Most jobs are on-campus, some relate to your field but others—like working in the library—could be more general.

Some colleges and universities don't participate in the work-study program, so check with the financial aid office to see if it's available and if you're eligible for it. It's good to apply early to have a better chance of getting the job you want most.

Since work-study is earned money (you do a job and get paid for it), this money does not need to be paid back. To learn more, check out https://student aid.ed.gov/sa/types/work-study.

Fellowships

Fellowships are another form of earned money that can be available to students. These are short-term positions in your field. They may focus on research, professional development, or working with a professor in your craft field. Most fellowships provide a stipend that covers some of the costs associated with your education, but are not enough to cover everything. While graduate students are more frequently granted fellowships than undergraduates are, there are some schools that give fellowships to undergrads.

Loans

There is always a gap between tuition and the amount of money you receive from a school in scholarships and grants. That gap is filled by student loans. Student loans have to be repaid. Interest varies depending on the type of loan. Be sure you understand how much interest you will be charged, when the interest starts to accumulate, and when you must start paying the loan back. Usually, repayment starts when you graduate or after a six-month grace period.

FEDERAL LOANS

Federal student loans are issued by the US government. They have lower interest rates and better repayment terms than other loans. You don't need anyone to cosign for your debt. If the loan is subsidized, the federal government pays the interest until you graduate. If it's unsubsidized, interest starts to accrue as soon as you accept the loan. That can amount to a very big difference in how much you pay for your education by the time the loan is paid off.

The most common federal student loan is the low-interest Federal Stafford Loan, which is available to both undergraduate and graduate students. Depending on household income, a student's Stafford loan might be subsidized or unsubsidized. (Note: the federal Perkins loan is no longer available.)

Most schools will require you to fill out the FAFSA when you apply for financial aid. FAFSA stands for Free Application for Federal Student Aid. Note that it doesn't say "free student aid." It says "free application." That means it does not cost anything to apply for federal student aid. You may get "offers" to submit the FAFSA for you for a fee—this is a scam. Don't do it.

PRIVATE LOANS

Chances are, federal student loans will not completely fill the gap between your tuition bill and any scholarships or grants you receive. Private student loans are issued by a bank or other financial institution. Rates of interest are generally higher than for federal loans, so be careful not to borrow more than you need. Eligibility criteria for private loans are based on your credit (and your cosigner's credit) history.

Don't just take the first loan you find. Do some research, compare interest rates and terms. Is the interest variable or fixed? Is there a cap on the variable interest? Is the company reputable? What are their repayment requirements?

INSTITUTIONAL LOANS

Many educational institutions make their own loans, using funds provided by donors such as alumni, corporations, and foundations, as well as from repayments made by prior college loan borrowers. Every college will have its own rules, terms, eligibility, and rates. Interest may be lower than private student loans, and the deferment option may be better, as well.

Learn more about all kinds of financial aid through the College Board website at http://bigfuture.collegeboard.org/pay-for-college.

FINANCIAL AID TIPS

- Some colleges/universities will offer tuition discounts to encourage students to attend—so tuition costs can be lower than they look at first.
- Apply for financial aid during your senior year of high school. The sooner you apply, the better your chances. Check out fafsa.gov to see how to get started.
- Compare offers from different schools—one school may be able to match or improve on another school's financial aid offer.
- Keep your grades up—a good GPA helps a lot when it comes to merit scholarships and grants.
- You have to reapply for financial aid every year, so you'll be filling out that FAFSA form again!
- Look for ways that loans might be deferred or forgiven—service commitment programs are a way to use service to pay back loans.

While You're in College

Of course, while you're enrolled in college, you'll take all the courses required for your major. Be sure to challenge yourself to learn new craft methods and techniques that you've never tried before.

There are also some other important subjects you can study while you're in college that will help you as a craft professional when you graduate. Consider taking additional course work in:

- Small business
- Marketing
- Public speaking

INTERNSHIPS AND VOLUNTEERING

An internship is a short-term job that provides some hands-on experience. An internship at a business related to your craft can provide experience and a chance to see how these businesses work. Some internships pay a small salary, but most are unpaid; instead, you will most likely be able to earn college credit for your internship.

To find an internship, you'll need to take action sooner rather than later! You may have competition for the internship you want, so the earlier you let people know you're interested, the better chance you have of being chosen:

- Talk to your adviser, the careers office, or the internship office to see if the school has a list of possible art internships or leads to find one.
- Put together a résumé showing what courses you've taken, jobs you've held, volunteer work you've done, and any honors you've received.
- Contact the place you'd like to work and ask if they offer internships for students and how you can apply for one.
- If the personal approach doesn't work, try an internet search for "internships" in your craft area
- An internship might also be an opportunity to travel—where do you want to go?

But remember:

- Do not pay a fee to any company who claims they will find you an internship if you pay them. You shouldn't have to pay for an unpaid job.
- If you can't afford to take a part-time job or a summer job without getting paid, then taking an unpaid internship may not be a good idea. Instead, see if the master craftsperson you want to learn from might hire you to help out over the summer.

Internships and apprenticeships let you learn one-to-one with a master artisan.
Steve Debenport/E+/Getty Images

Apprenticeship

For all of recorded time, the way craftspeople and artisans learned their crafts was through apprenticeship. This method was divided during the Middle Ages into three categories:

- *Apprentice:* A "learner" who would work under a master artisan to learn the trade. The apprentice (who often started in childhood) was not paid, but lived in the master's household, worked for the master, and learned the trade.
- *Journeyman:* A tradesman who knew the job but still worked under the master's supervision. A journeyman would be paid a daily wage and often traveled to other workshops in other towns for a day or so. A journeyman was more than a beginner, but not yet a master.
- *Master:* To qualify as a master, the craftsperson would have to produce a "masterpiece" that met the requirements of the guild for that craft or trade. Only after demonstrating "mastery" in the craft could an artisan

be considered fully qualified, and able to set up an independent shop and take on apprentices.

Today, the term "apprenticeship" is used in many types of businesses. The US Department of Labor (DOL) defines apprenticeship as "an employer-driven, 'learn-while-you-earn' model that combines on-the-job training, provided by the employer that hires the apprentice, with job-related instruction in curricula tied to the attainment of national skills standards."[2]

According to the DOL, there are five basic components of a typical formal apprenticeship:

- *Business involvement:* Employers are the foundation of every apprenticeship program. They play an active role in building the program and remain involved every step of the way. Employers frequently work together through apprenticeship councils, industry associations, or other partnerships to share the administrative tasks involved in maintaining apprenticeship programs.
- *Structured on-the-job training:* Apprenticeships always include an on-the-job training component. Apprentices receive hands-on training from an experienced mentor at the job site. On-the-job training focuses on the skills and knowledge an apprentice must learn during the program to be fully proficient on the job. This training is based on national industry standards, customized to the needs of the particular employer.
- *Related instruction:* One of the unique aspects of apprenticeships is that they combine on-the-job learning with related instruction on the technical and academic competencies that apply to the job. Education partners collaborate with business to develop the curriculum, which often incorporates established national-level skill standards. The related instruction may be provided by community colleges, technical schools, or apprenticeship training schools—or by the business itself. It can be delivered at a school, online, or at the job site.
- *Rewards for skill gains:* Apprentices receive wages when they begin work and receive pay increases as they meet benchmarks for skill attainment. This helps reward and motivate apprentices as they advance through their training.
- *Nationally recognized credential:* Every graduate of an apprenticeship program receives a nationally recognized credential. This is a portable

credential that signifies to employers that apprentices are fully qualified for the job.³

You can find a lot of information about apprenticeships at www.dol.gov /apprenticeship and www.apprenticeship.gov.

SURAYIA HOWERTER—BLACKSMITH

Sue Howerter.
Courtesy of Sue Howerter

Sue Howerter began working for the city of Austin, Texas, as a gravedigger. As she moved up through various jobs with the city, she went on to earn a master's degree in applied geography with a specialty in environmental studies from Texas State University–San Marcos. After taking a class for her own enjoyment, she fell in love with blacksmithing. Today, she has her own forge and works as an artist-blacksmith full time. She is a board member of Balcones Forge, a nonprofit blacksmith organization affiliated with Artist-Blacksmith's Association of North America (ABANA). Her work can be seen on their website at www.balconesforge.org/suemurray.

How did you become interested in blacksmithing?

About 1999, I went to the Austin Community College (ACC) welding department to take a continuing education welding class after work so I could make cool, funky stuff for my garden. When I got there, I saw they had a whole shop and a blacksmithing program under the auspices of art metal. Now it's actually a degree program. Once I saw the anvils and the forges, I thought, man! I've got to try that! Once I did I was hooked that minute.

How did you learn blacksmithing?

I got a lot of training after work at ACC through 2002. I also joined Balcones Forge. I started meeting with the guys and gals at someone's shop or at events we're doing for the public. I started going to our workshops with blacksmiths doing ornamental iron. I took classes until I decided to set up my own shop. I learned from the other smiths at Balcones Forge, taking workshops, then setting up a shop and doing it. There are so many good resources, depending where you live. We have more resources than people would know—especially now that there are so many. I've been a member of ABANA since about 2000, I've gone to some of their conferences, seen some really amazing work, and got some amazing ideas. They have one magazine that highlights all the different kinds of blacksmiths, *The Anvil's Ring*, and another, *The Hammer's Blow*, that is how-to instruction. They put out a lot of information through the year. They've been a great source of information, for sure.

What is a typical day on your job?

Since my shop is out back of my house, it's take a cup of coffee and go out to the shop, decide what I'm working on and get to it. In the summer, I try to do my hot work before lunch, because it gets really hot here. I've got an open shop that's not temperature controlled.

What's the best part of your job?

Being able to do what I want like I want. I do have a lot of free range, because I do my job to supplement retirement at this point, so I'm out there working all the time, but I can pick and choose my projects and my customers a little bit easier, because it doesn't put the roof over my head. I'm out there all the time like a regular job. I can skip a weekday and do a weekend day—you have a lot more flexibility.

What's the most challenging part of your job?

For me, it is deciding how best to get my work out and price it. That's extremely challenging. My sister's an artist, too, and it is an issue. There are quite a few black-smiths that'll teach because it keeps the money coming in. I don't teach, but I did do my first workshop in Mississippi—it was great. But for me, pricing my work and get-

ting it out there is so hard. I like making some things that take a lot of time, a lot of detailing, a lot of punchwork, but you can price yourself out of the market when you start adding up time. The materials are a lot less costly than the amount of time you put it into it. Doing this as a retirement business, I can do it a little differently from someone who needs to crank work out so they can pay the bills. I've also found that if you're to make a living at it, you need

A working guitar. *Courtesy of Sue Howerter*

to also be a welder/fabricator because welding will significantly reduce the time involved. There are some professionals who don't have to worry about that because they're working with extremely high-end clients, but most of the blacksmiths I know have to choose between where something's welded and where it's forged. I don't weld, so if I need something welded I need to ask a friend to do it.

What's the most surprising thing about your job?

It's a variety of things. I've been surprised that I've had clients that have been more than willing to let me do my thing with minimal input—they want my thing, my style. People end up recognizing my work somewhere, because of my style, and that's pretty neat.

What's your educational background? Did your education prepare you for the job?

I have a master's degree in applied geography with a specialty in environmental studies from Texas State University–San Marcos. I've been probably blacksmithing longer than I used that degree in my career. I've been retired about thirteen years. I retired at forty-seven so I could work in my blacksmith shop.

Is the job what you expected?

It's a lot more than what I expected. I don't know that I knew what to expect. It's one of those things where you can never know everything. You'll be learning until you don't do it anymore, and then some. I've seen things made by blacksmiths that I never would have thought were made by blacksmiths. Just the things you can do with metal that you never would think you could. It challenges me every day. You have to take some steps before you can take other steps—sometimes you have to start again because you can't get there.

How do clients find you?

I don't have a website. I'm just not good at that electronic stuff. One client found me through Balcones Forge, and contacted me through the president of the organization. I've been showing for quite a few years now at a big show for master gardeners—I've gotten some projects through them as well. Or I'll have someone who meets me at a market and asks if I can do certain types of work. A lot of times people need something but they don't know where to find a blacksmith, so if it's not something I do, I'll try to point them in the direction of someone who does do that kind of work.

What is it like to work with clients on a commission?

I've had some really nice clients who are willing to let me do my thing. And then they're pleasantly surprised that they end up liking it even better than they thought they would. That's very rewarding. Usually they have a project in mind—like a driveway gate with a big oak tree on it. We meet, we talk about what they're wanting, we go to the site and measure, we go back and design something, meet again to see if that's what they're thinking. Depending on how complicated it is, some blacksmiths charge for their drawing. With the clients I've had, I haven't felt like I've had to do that. We try to put together how many hours we think it'll take, then you have to figure out an additional percentage, because it's always going to take you longer than you think. Pricing work is always a huge thing, you have to figure out what your overhead is, what you think you need per hour, and try to work from there.

What's next? Where do you see yourself going from here?

I don't have a strict plan. I think about it a lot—I'm always learning new things or wanting to try something different. I'm talking with another blacksmith about doing joint projects to put in a gallery. I'd like to get a little more detailed, more complex with the things I'm making, different joinery than I usually use, just so I can be a better blacksmith. I'd be considered an artist blacksmith, because I don't do tools and farm implements. I do try to make things that have a purpose. Sometimes people feel more justified in spending the money on something that has a use.

Where do you see the field going from here?

Since there are so many different types of blacksmithing, it's hard to say. There are so many specialties people can focus on. They can be an artist, or focus on railings or fireplace screens, there are farriers who also do ornamental work or teach classes. Because of the TV shows like *Forged in Fire*, people are seeing that there are more kinds of things they can do and know. It also depends on what part of the country you're in—some places up north that are older will have a lot of restoration work. There's more artistic work, more knife makers. It's probably something that would be worked into other projects, now, like architectural iron work, just because people know it's there.

How can a young person prepare for this career while in high school?

A lot of industrial arts programs have been closed down, but some are starting back up. When I was in school, you could do arc welding or other trade programs. Or they would have been part of Future Farmers of America or take shop classes. Not everyone wants to go to college and do that kind of thing. Some of the schools here have welding programs and participate in state and national competitions, so they have the opportunity to see what other kids are doing and earn high school welding certifications. We have kids who come out to our Balcones Forge meetings because they're interested in knife making and then learn there are other things, too. ACC has a whole degree program now, with designing and then making what you design, techniques, power hammer, tool making.

What is your advice for a young person considering this career?

Take advantage of any opportunity to take a class that's in any kind of way related. Look first for high school trade programs, industrial arts programs, or art programs that teach you how to draw something out. Look for community college programs or craft schools that offer blacksmith programs. Or find your local blacksmith organization or guild. There are a lot more than you'd think! Go to meetings—you don't necessarily have

A small sculpture of a butterfly.
Courtesy of Sue Howerter

to be a member to go to a meeting. There are professionals you can learn from. It wouldn't hurt to learn business and finance stuff for your own benefit. You can start and sell at a weekend market and see how it goes with little stuff before you make it a business. We have people who come in with all kinds of experience, it might be art or barbecue forks or what have you. They all have techniques, and ways of doing things, or tools—it generates questions in your own brain about what options are out there. There's all kinds of jobs—the sky's the limit once you get some skills.

Pursuing a Professional Craft Art Career

All the hard work pays off when you make your craft art business successful.
pixdeluxe/E+/Getty Images

The Business of Craft Art

Craft artists need to think like entrepreneurs in order to run successful craft businesses. But what does that mean? Basically, it means understanding what goes into running your business and making sure those things get done.

Your Entrepreneurial Plan

As an entrepreneur you will need to make a plan that covers:

> Your work is going to fill a large part of your life, and the only way to be truly satisfied is to do what you believe is great work. And the only way to do great work is to love what you do. If you haven't found it yet, keep looking. Don't settle. As with all matters of the heart, you'll know when you find it. And, like any great relationship, it just gets better and better as the years roll on.—Steve Jobs[1]

THE MARKET

Is there a demand for what you make? How can you find out? The US Small Business Administration recommends browsing craft shows and online craft marketplaces to "[s]ee what's already out there in your niche. Look to see if your items fit into an existing product category (there's likely demand), but there aren't a gazillion sellers selling very similar items (too much competition for the same thing)."[2]

Craft artists are entrepreneurs who need business skills. *Eva-Katalin/E+/Getty Images*

YOUR STYLE

What makes your craft art different from other people who make similar work? Your style is what makes your work unique. But also think about what materials you use, the quality of your work, and other things that make your work stand out from the crowd.

YOUR IDEAL CUSTOMER

Imagine the person who is going to love what you make. Who are they? What's important to them? How does your work match what they're looking for/dreaming of?

YOUR BUSINESS NAME

The US Small Business Administration recommends: "Pick a business name that appeals to buyers and communicates what you sell. Don't get too obscure. Pick something with meaning and strong brand potential—catchy is good. Be sure to check the name's availability. An attorney can guide you through the legal process to secure your business name."[3]

YOUR TIME

- How much profit do you need to consider yourself successful? This number may be low at first but will go up during your lifetime as you grow into having a family and a home. Find out what other craft artists consider normal.
- How much time can you physically spend working? Some crafts are physically very hard, and you need to know how many hours you can reasonably expect to spend on making.
- How much time do you need to spend on the business side? Estimates vary, but it's reasonable to expect to spend 50 percent of your time on business.
- How much time do you need to travel, hang out, let your mind wander? For a creative person, this is not just wasting time. This is important to

resting your brain and letting your creative ideas form in the back of your mind. You *need* to spend time "doing nothing." Be sure to leave enough time for it!

YOUR COSTS

You will need to keep track of your costs on a *regular basis*. Know what you can expect to spend money on:

- *Equipment:* What special equipment will you need to make what you make?
- *Space:* Where will you work? Do you need a designated studio or workshop? Where will you store finished pieces? Where will you take care of business?
- *Materials:* What materials do you need to make your work? What do they cost? Can you save money if you make bulk purchases? Do you have a reliable supplier?
- *Getting the work out there:* What do you need to spend on marketing and promotion, website, travel, booth fees, stockists' commissions? How do online marketplaces like Etsy compare to setting up a booth at a craft fair?
- *Taxes:* Whatever you do, do not fall behind in paying your taxes. Many small businesses go bankrupt because the owner thought paying taxes could happen after paying everyone else. It doesn't work like that. See the section on taxes later in this chapter.

Promoting Your Craft Art Business

Artisans can be uncomfortable with terms like "promoting" or "marketing," but as a professional craft artist, letting people get to know your artwork is part of your job. There are certain things you should always have ready, so you can respond to opportunities as they come up. You don't want to be left scrambling to pull things together at the last minute!

KEEPING UP WITH YOUR PAPERWORK

To keep track of your craft artist business, you'll need to understand where you are and where you're going. These types of records will help you do that.

INCOME STATEMENT

This is also called a profit-and-loss or P&L statement. This is where you track all your income and expenses for the quarter and for the year. At the bottom (the "bottom line"), you subtract expenses from income. If the number is positive, you've made a net profit. If the number is negative, you've made a net loss.

BALANCE SHEET

A balance sheet is a statement of the assets (what you own), liabilities (what you owe), and capital (the difference between assets and liabilities) at a particular point in time.

CASH FLOW STATEMENT

This is where you track cash in and cash out. This is how you keep track of your ability to meet your financial obligations on a day-to-day basis.

Of course, this is just a short introduction. Be sure to read books on small business and entrepreneurship for artists and artisans, take classes, and become an expert on running your business. Sometimes it may be worth the cost to hire a bookkeeper or accountant to help you track your finances.

Photographs of Your Work

It is very important to have excellent photographs of your artwork that show each piece to its best advantage. If you're a good photographer, you can learn how to take photos of your work yourself. But it's a tricky process to get the light just right, especially for three-dimensional objects. Many craft artists find it's better to hire a photographer who has specific expertise in photographing 3-D work. Prices vary, so you'll need to do your homework to find an affordable photographer in your area. The best way is to talk with other craft artists as well as local galleries and museums to discover which photographers they recommend.

Creativity and vision balance technical and business skills. *JGalione/E+/Getty Images*

You'll need to have both high- and low-resolution images:

- High-resolution (300 dpi) images between 5,000 and 10,000 KB. TIFF files have the most information, so you should have them, but you will usually submit JPG files. JPG files are compressed and lose a little information when saved, while TIFF files are not compressed. High-res images are used for print (such as catalogs, exhibition announcements, magazines, posters, printed ads, etc.).
- Low-resolution (72 dpi) files are used online, for your website and social media, and to e-mail to prospective stockists and collectors. Low-res files are smaller, so they upload and download much more quickly than high-res files. Use an image program like Adobe Photoshop or something similar to save copies of your high-res JPG files as low-res JPG files.

The photos themselves *must* be:

- True to the color of the original artwork
- In focus
- Free of hotspots and shadows

- Cropped to the edges (no background showing) for 2-D work
- Against a plain background for 3-D work

- Detail images are closeup photos that show particular aspects of a piece.

Your Online Presence

The internet is an important tool for advocating for your work. Your website is your online portfolio. Your Instagram, Twitter, and other social media accounts are where you tell your story. And your mailing list is how you keep your best customers and fans up-to-date on what you're doing, where you'll be, and what's new in your work.

YOUR WEBSITE

Every craft artist needs a website. Your website is your online portfolio. It's the place to showcase your work in an organized way for the world to see. Shop around for the website platform that meets your needs best. For instance, free sites are available but may require you to include their name in your URL. If you want to sell work directly from your site, you may want to get a site with an e-commerce option and you'll want to list prices for your pieces. If you only sell work through stockists, do not list your prices but do include direct links to those stockists so people can find your pieces and buy them.

In general, your website should contain:

- Home page with links to the other pages.
- About page with your story: your background, what you make, why you make it, etc.
- Contact page with a form visitors can use to get in touch with you. Be sure to use a captcha code to keep out the robots (be aware that even with a form and a captcha code, you will be contacted by scammers through your contact page from time to time). This is an important part of your customer relations. *Be sure to answer these contact e-mails right away!*

- Portfolio pages for each series you want to show and information about individual pieces, including how to acquire them.
- News page that shows what you're doing and where you'll be next (fairs, trunk shows, demonstrations, etc.)
- Link to sign up for your e-newsletter (see "Your Mailing List," below)

Keep the design of your site clear and simple. Think about it from the visitor's point of view and make it easy to navigate. Avoid things that move and jump around, and anything noisy (including music) that starts immediately on its own. If you want to include videos that show you working or giving a demonstration, set them to start when the visitor clicks play—not on their own.

YOUR SOCIAL MEDIA

Social media accounts are the place to show your latest work, works in progress, announce your news, and follow other craft artists, stockists, and influencers. At the time of writing, most craft artists like Instagram because it's all about images. But Twitter also accepts images, and if you can keep your comments short, Twitter can be a useful way to share your work as well. Some artists have Facebook pages, but Instagram and Twitter will reach a much wider audience.

Social media changes too quickly for any tips given here to stay relevant. You'll want to keep informed about those changes and about expert recommendations for craft artists using social media. However, there are some general points:

- Post images frequently.
- Post high-quality low-resolution images. These can include finished work, work in progress, video of you in the studio, photos or videos of exhibitions you're in, artwork in museums that you like with your comments.
- Only post selfies if they are relevant to your life and work as a craft artist.
- Use relevant hashtags.
- Follow other craft artists of all kinds as well as galleries, interior designers, architects, and the people you already know.
- Comment on others' posts.

- Don't pay for followers—there are always people who offer to connect you to thousands of followers, but those aren't real followers. They aren't people who are following you because they're interested in your work. (Most of them aren't people at all.)

YOUR MAILING LIST

Your mailing list consists of people who have expressed an interest in your work or who might be interested in your work. Your list should include names, mailing addresses, and e-mail addresses. If you can include phone numbers and notes on who the person is and why they're on the list, so much the better. Possible categories could be:

- Your friends and family
- People in your local arts and crafts community
- People who have signed up to be on your mailing list
- Anyone who ever handed you a business card
- Movers and shakers in your community
- Members of arts organization boards
- Other artists, craft artists, and artisans in the community

You can keep the list yourself in a spreadsheet program like Excel or Google Sheets, or you can keep it online in an e-mail marketing site like MailChimp or ConstantContact. If you use a site like MailChimp or ConstantContact, you can send an e-mail newsletter to your mailing list monthly, quarterly, or whenever you have news. At the time of writing, MailChimp is free and allows as many images as you're likely to need to upload.

You might also want to keep a postcard list, with names and addresses of people you'd like to invite to special events. This can include the people on your mailing list and others that are postcard list only for whatever reason.

Keep track of your mailing list, and make sure it's as current as you can make it. This will take time, but it's worth it. The people who sign up for your mailing list through your website are your best followers. They have chosen to be there!

Sales

As we saw in chapter 2, there are many different venues for selling your work. Think carefully about which type of sales strategy works best for your work and for your personality.

For instance, if you are extroverted and energetic, a long-weekend craft show can be a wonderful, exciting, motivating opportunity to meet potential customers and see how they respond to your work. If you're more introverted, that same situation could seem like a little slice of hell.

Likewise, if you make a few, perfect pieces every year that each require hours and hours of careful, precise work, you might be happier and more comfortable working on commission than trying to fulfill wholesale orders. But if you are good at production work and can make lots and lots of the same piece quickly and easily, wholesale orders could be the way to go for you.

> I think it's always good to first go to the store and see their products to see if your art works in that store or gallery. I don't believe in oversaturating my product —I like to be selective about where my work is shown.—Suzanne Wang, ceramic artist

Shipping

Here's some great advice from the US Small Business Administration: "If any part of your business includes selling online, consider the shipping. Prompt and reliable shipping plays a huge role in getting good customer reviews. So compare prices and find a shipping provider, whether you go with USPS, UPS or FedEx. Then invest in good packing materials to avoid breakage."[4]

SELLING CRAFTS ONLINE

Having an online presence is more than just your website. Here are some of the top websites for selling craft arts:

Etsy	iCraft
E-bay	I Made It Market
eCrater	Made It Myself
Alibaba	Maker Faire
Artfire	Meylah
Artflock	Misi (UK)
Bonanza	Renegade Crafft
Dawanda	SilkFair
Foodzie	Sourcing Handmade
Free Craft Fair	Supermarket
GLC Arts and Crafts Mall	Zibbet
Handmade Artists' Shop	

Things Every Self-Employed Person Needs to Know

Whether you're a craft artist or any other kind of independent, self-employed person, there are some very important things that you need to take care of for yourself. When you work for an employer, they are often responsible for making sure that you have health, life, and disability insurance, vacation and sick leave, and a retirement plan. Self-employed people must stay on top of all those things for themselves (and for their employees, if they have any).

Insurance

As a self-employed small-businessperson, there are several types of insurance you will need.

- *Health insurance:* The average monthly cost of an individual health insurance plan is $440 for an individual and $1,168 for a family.[5] This amount depends on things like which plan you choose, how much your deductible is, how much your copay amounts are, and other factors. It's important to look at all your options and make a careful decision.

- *Auto insurance:* If you have a car or motorcycle, you have to have insurance. If you use your vehicle for your business, keep track of your mileage, because you can deduct some of your car expenses from your income tax.

- *Disability insurance:* If you get hurt or sick and can't work, disability insurance pays a percentage of your regular income. Keep good records, because you have to be able to prove how much money you make in a month or a year. There are both short- and long-term disability insurance policies.

- *Life insurance:* If you have dependents (like a spouse and/or children), then you need life insurance to help replace your income if you should die. Also, if you want to borrow money for your business, the bank may require you to have life insurance.[6]

- *Liability insurance:* Depending on your situation, there are several kinds of liability insurance that might be relevant for your business: product liability, negligence, and personal injury are the main ones to look into.

- *Business insurance:* Small businesses with employees usually need a comprehensive policy combining property and liability coverage, to protect the business structure itself and any business-related equipment against theft or damage, and if an employee or someone else is injured on your premises.

I never took out a loan for my business—I only would spend money I had. I never had credit card debt I couldn't pay the next month. I would live within my means. The business grew every year. I was grateful that every year seemed to be better than the next—there were some ups and downs. I would recommend that to anyone in life in general, but especially in this kind of work. Use good judgment and don't get in over your head.—Tom Kuhner, jeweler

Save money. Professional artists, we don't get sick leave, paid vacation, a retirement fund. Either meet a significant other with a retirement fund or keep tattooing until your body gives out.—Manny Vega, tattoo artist

Saving for the Future

When you're young and first starting out in life, it often seems more important to focus on paying your immediate expenses. Retirement seems so far in the future. That's for your grandparents to think about! Why should it matter to you?

Well, for one thing, the future arrives a lot faster than you expect it. The other reason is that the sooner you start saving for retirement, the more money you'll have when you retire. Let's take a quick look at the difference between starting to save now and waiting a while (this book is not a substitute for expert financial or legal advice).

There are several kinds of retirement plans that individuals can participate in. Here's a short list to give you an idea of what to look into. Bear in mind that these things can change all the time, so there may be more or fewer options with different rules and regulations when you're ready to start. The following list is adapted from the website NerdWallet:

1. *Traditional or Roth IRA*: Best for those just starting out, or saving less than $6,000 a year. If you're leaving a job to start a business, you can also roll your old 401(k) into an IRA. Tax deduction on contributions to a traditional IRA; no immediate deduction for Roth IRA, but withdrawals in retirement are tax-free.

2. *Solo 401(k)*: Best for a business owner or self-employed person with no employees (except a spouse, if applicable).

3. *SEP IRA*: Best for self-employed people or small-business owners with no or few employees.

4. *SIMPLE IRA*: Best for larger businesses, with up to one hundred employees.

5. *Defined benefit plan*: Best for a self-employed person with no employees who has a high income and wants to save a lot for retirement on an ongoing basis.[7]

Let's take a look at the difference between saving and not saving, in some different scenarios from Calculator.net.[8]

				Compare Starting a Traditional, SIMPLE, or SEP IRA (pre-tax $) by Age			
	Annual Contribution	Annual Rate of Return	Retirement Age 65	After Tax at Age 65	Equal to Today's
Age 20	$1,200 ($100/month)	6%	$256,669	$218,168	$57,692
Age 20	$6,000 (annual limit)	6%	$1,277,838	$1,086,162	$287,223
Age 30	$1,200 ($100/month)	6%	$134,490	$114,317	$40,626
Age 30	$6,000 (annual limit)	6%	$669,377	$568,971	$202,203
Age 40	$1,200 ($100/month)	6%	$66,267	$56,327	$26,902
Age 40	$6,000 (annual limit)	6%	$329,616	$280,174	$133,813

We're using a 6 percent annual rate of return because it's a very conservative (low) estimate compared to the types of returns real IRA accounts have been earning in recent decades. The important things to notice are:

1. The difference between contributing $100 a month (for a total of $1,200 per year) and contributing the full allowed amount ($6,000 per year)
2. The difference at age 65 between starting savings in your 20s and starting in your 40s

Another thing an employer often provides is matching funds for a 401(k) retirement fund. For instance, if you contribute 10 percent of your salary to your 401(k), your employer might contribute up to another 10 percent, for a total of 20 percent. But when you're self-employed, you have to fund that match yourself. So aim to contribute about 20 percent of your income or more (up to the total allowed) to your retirement fund. If you really can't afford that at first, begin with $100 a month and then raise the contribution as your income goes up over the years.

How can you afford to do that? It's simple, once you accept the idea to *pay yourself first*. Google that phrase and you'll find hundreds of reputable investment advisers who recommend this process. If you put that $100 (or $500) into your IRA *first*, before you pay any other bills or buy something you want, *you won't even miss it*. And it will be in your IRA, quietly earning you money until you need it when you retire.

Taxes

Paying your taxes is part of running a business. Some people object to paying taxes, but taxes are legally required. (If you think of it as doing your part to contribute to the shared resources of your community, it stings less.) Since tax laws are constantly changing, it will be your responsibility to keep track of what you are supposed to pay to whom, when, how much, and how often. An accountant or tax attorney can help you, if you need help.

In general, you'll need to be responsible for the following.

FEDERAL INCOME TAX

Self-employed people are responsible for making quarterly payments toward their own federal income tax. You must also pay self-employment tax to cover your Social Security and Medicare taxes (when you work for an employer, they deduct this from your paycheck automatically).

Do not miss this important step! You can find everything you need to know about paying taxes as a sole proprietor or an independent contractor at the IRS's Self-Employed Individuals Tax Center page.[9]

STATE INCOME TAX

Some states charge state income tax and some don't. If you itemize your federal income tax, you may be able to deduct your state income tax from your federal income tax. Be sure you understand the rules in your state.

SALES TAX

Sales tax is determined on a state-by-state basis. You need to know whether you must charge sales tax in your state. Recently, tax laws for selling online have been changing in terms of whether to charge sales tax or not. Be sure you know the expectations for all of your sales venues, and be sure to factor in the cost of sales tax in your own accounting.

LIZ GRACE—WOODWORKER

Liz Grace. *Photo by Amy Wilson. Courtesy of Liz Grace*

Liz Grace runs River's Bend Woodworking Studio in Plymouth, New Hampshire. She was juried into the New Hampshire Woodworkers Guild at the emerging artist level and is a juried member of the League of New Hampshire Craftsmen. She also holds bachelor's and master's degrees in agronomy from the University of New Hampshire. Her furniture reflects the clean lines and simplicity of the Shaker tradition as well as the Japanese aesthetic tradition. Her website at www.riversbendwood. com includes pictures and stories of the furniture she makes.

How did you become interested in woodworking?

It goes back to my early childhood playing with wood. It fascinated me and I loved the smell of it. In junior high and high school, I wanted to take woodworking, but I wasn't allowed to because "boys took woodworking and girls took home ec." I used to look in the windows and wish I was in there! I went to three different high schools. At the second one [after a lengthy interrogation by the guidance counselor and the shop teacher], I was told that if I passed the small-engine machine class first, I might be able to take woodworking. They thought that would deter me, but I loved it! The next year, I went to a different school that didn't let me take shop classes because I was on the "college track." So I found some local cabinet shops and asked to be an apprentice, but was told, "No, you're a girl." After I graduated, woodworking became a hobby. I decided to teach myself, which was probably really dangerous—but I still have all ten fingers!

What is a typical day on your job?

I try to come in to the shop around 8:00 or 8:30 a.m. Then I plan how I'm going to lay out my work for efficiency of time. I'll take a break for lunch and work until 5:00 or 6:00 p.m. As an entrepreneur, you have to work more hours than you'd think. I do try to take Sundays off. And there are days when you have to get other stuff done—meetings, errands—but that's my basic work routine.

What's the best part of your job?

The whole creative process—I love that part! It can very daunting, as with any creative thing. You can have a lot of doubts. I also really enjoy working for myself. You need self-discipline and the ability to structure your time.

What's the most challenging part of your job?

Business. That's something I've spent a lot of time to learn—how to market, how to sell, how to engage with customers. I make custom pieces, so I'm working with the customer one-to-one to try to realize their dream with my creativity.

What's the most surprising thing about your job?

I'm surprised by everything at one level. I was surprised and pleased to find how willing other woodworkers are to share their knowledge and skills with someone just starting out. I've found that woodworkers are very open, generous, giving of their time. They're noncompetitive in that way.

Did your education prepare you for the job?

It must have—I'm here! We're all where we are by all the experiences we have. I never had formal education in arts, crafts, or woodworking. I've taken classes at woodworking schools for one or two weeks at a time. I chose those for who the instructor was and the topic being taught. If you can learn from somebody else, the learning curve is much more rapidly achieved. You still have to figure out how *you're* going to do it. One thing having a degree does is show that you have the motivation and tenacity to do what you set out to do—to yourself as well as others. You learn how to dig around and find the information you need. Even if your degree is in something else, you'll be applying those skills you learned along the way.

Is the job what you expected?

Yes and no. I was ideological—I'm going to make a cool thing out of wood. The reality is you have to work hard and know the business aspects. There's a lot of structure that has to support it. Some artists don't want to learn business because they think it will hinder their creativity. But it opens the door to more customers and, therefore, more creativity.

What's next? Where do you see yourself going from here?

Up! I was juried into the New Hampshire Furniture Masters at the emerging artist level. My goal is to become a furniture master. I want to keep improving my skills to bring the creative ideas I have to life and to form. That's a big part of being a craftsperson—you have to get your skills to the point where you can realize your ideas. I have a lot to learn, and I look forward to learning it.

Where do you see the field of woodworking going from here?

There are a number of dynamics that are happening now. I think the current generation of people who would buy furniture are desiring to live a more modest life with less furniture. There's a focus on smaller homes with multifunctional furniture that uses wood and other materials. I also see an increase in cultural valuation of something made by hand, because so few people do it and have the ability to do it.

How can a young person prepare for this career while in high school?

Find a mentor if you can—a neighbor, a teacher—they don't have to be a professional woodworker if they know a lot about woodworking. There are summer programs. Experiment on your own—you can learn a lot with hand tools. That's how I started. There are books, YouTube (some of it's good, some is junk—you want to be careful). And you can start looking into schools like the Center for Furniture Craftsmanship in Rockport, Maine, or the Penland School of Crafts in North Carolina.

What is your advice for a young person considering this career?

Try it as a hobby on weekends and evenings to see how you like it. If you find your interest stays, just keep following that interest. Expose yourself to a lot of art and artists, learn how to draw and to work in three dimensions. Drawing is how you develop your eye-hand coordination. But mostly, experiment.

MICHAEL HOPKO—GLASS ARTIST

Mike Hopko. *Courtesy of Michael Hopko*

Michael Hopko is a glassblower in Weaverville, in the Trinity Alps region of Northern California. He is best known for his fish and octopus series, which are available in galleries all over the United States. Hopko Art Glass can be found online at www.hopko artglass.com.

How did you become interested in glassblowing?

The first time I saw glassblowing was at a Shasta College. I'd done ceramics in high school. My mom's an art teacher and I was raised doing art. I got into Shasta College and was taking ceramics and random other classes. I didn't even really know what glass was but they had a hot glass studio and that's where I started. This was 1991.

What is a typical day on your job?

I have my studio right next to my home. I get up about 5:00 a.m. to beat the heat. I fire up the glory hole and open the annealer to let the heat out. The morning is getting ready for the day. It takes about an hour to get everything working. My assistant will show up about forty-five minutes later and do the prep for the studio. Then I start working. I'm a wholesale artist, for the most part—I ship to galleries and shops around the country, so I have a list of things to make and my priorities. We play music all day every day. I'm tired at the end of the day—whether it's octopus or fish.

What's the best part of your job?

The satisfaction that I get to do something that's really a luxury to everyone. The fact that people appreciate what I do to the point that I make a living off it. I really enjoy what I do physically—I get to play with glass every day. Sometimes it's a "job" but I mostly really enjoy it. I like to hone my skills and make everything the best that I can. And people are supporting what I like to do.

What's the most challenging part of your job?

Pushing through the hard days when you don't quite feel 100 percent. I have three employees. Being a boss, running a business, having people counting on you so they get their paychecks—that can be a challenge. I have helpers, but I have to be here to make it all happen.

What's the most surprising thing about your job?

That it keeps going and going and going! I've been in business since 1997 at twenty-five years old. I quit all my jobs and built the studio on my grandparents' property in a small shed that we built on to. It's been a long journey to get to here. A glass shop is a lot of work—once you fire the furnace up. You're always trying to make things you can make money from as well as be creative at the same time. There's not a lot of the luxury of just messing around.

Did your education prepare you for the job?

Not necessarily. I learned more about how to run a business in the six or seven years when I worked for other people. It definitely got my foot in the door. I was at Shasta College for two years but never got a degree. My art teacher got me a job working in a studio in Nevada City, California. That's where I picked up the practical experience to make it all work. They don't teach you production—art school is one thing, but there's no necessity to figure out how to make it pay. My first jobs were production work and that trained me to be efficient, so I didn't waste a lot of time and energy, which is key to keeping going.

Is the job what you expected?

Probably more now that I'm at this point. I feel very lucky to be where I am and to be appreciated at this point. I'm basically what you call a blue-collar artist. I've been working to refine my skills so that regardless of where I came from, people who know about glass appreciate what I do.

What's next, where do you see yourself going from here?

Right now I'm just happy to be working. I suffered a major medical issue in January so I'm just glad to be alive. I feel refreshed and reset. I'd like to make less pieces and do some more education, do an internship at a glass school and teach a few classes. It's something I've been thinking about. I've got tons of work to do, I'm back

Glass octopus by Michael Hopko. *Courtesy of Michael Hopko*

up with orders and things are going good. You've got to want it to get up in the dark and keep things going.

Where do you see the field going from here?

I've seen it declining for the last twenty years. I almost feel like I'm part of the end. With art, you've got to be there to see it and want it and buy it. We seem to be pushing away from retail shopping but we're sort of in a lull right now, with everyone spending their time staring at a screen. Everything I make uses natural resources and has to be mined somewhere else. It kind of seems like the end of an era. But who knows?

What is your advice for a young person considering this career?

You've got to work hard at it. There's no easy road, no easy way there. To work for other people who are successful is the best way to start after you finish your schooling, because you can get a lot of insight into how to make it happen. If you want to be a teacher, that's a whole different road. But to run a full-time studio and support yourself doing it, you want to get your experience with someone who's already doing it. That's also how you get enough time to build the skills you're going to need. Glass is a repetitive thing and you have to spend hours to be consistent and get things to come out the way you want.

Notes

Introduction

1. Patrick Rothfuss, *The Wise Man's Fear*, Kingkiller Chronicle #2 (New York: DAW Books, 2011, 1043.
2. Richard Glover, "Principles of Great Design: Craftsmanship," *Smashing*, January 13, 2010, https://www.smashingmagazine.com/2010/01/principles-of-great-design-craftsmanship/.
3. Todd Oppenheimer and the Craftsmanship Initiative Team, Craftsmanship Initiative, https://craftsmanship.net/the-initiative/overview/.
4. David Kiersey, "Portrait of an Artisan," The Keirsey Group, https://keirsey.com/temperament/artisan-overview/.

Chapter 1

1. Michael Gungor, *The Crowd, the Critic and the Muse: A Book for Creators* (Denver, CO: Woodsley Press, 2012).
2. US Bureau of Labor Statistics, "Craft and Fine Artists," https://www.bls.gov/ooh/arts-and-design/craft-and-fine-artists.htm.
3. The Art Career Project, "Blacksmith," https://www.theartcareerproject.com/careers/blacksmith/.
4. Chegg CareerMatch, "Career Insights: How Much Does a Tattoo Artist Make?" https://www.careermatch.com/job-prep/career-insights/articles/how-much-does-a-tattoo-artist-make/.
5. The Art Career Project, "Tattoo Artist," https://www.theartcareerproject.com/become/tattoo-artist/.
6. The Art Career Project, "How to Become a Jewelry Designer," https://www.theartcareerproject.com/become/jewelry-designer/.

7. US Bureau of Labor Statistics, "Jewelers and Precious Stone and Metal Workers: Pay," https://www.bls.gov/ooh/production/jewelers-and-precious-stone-and-metal-workers.htm#tab-5.

8. US Bureau of Labor Statistics, "What Jewelers and Precious Stone and Metal Workers Do," https://www.bls.gov/ooh/production/jewelers-and-precious-stone-and-metal-workers.htm#tab-2.

Chapter 2

1. *Handmade Business*, "Craft Show Listings," http://handmade-business.com/craft-show-listings/.

2. Jane Hammill, "What Is a Trunk Show and How Do I Make One Work for Me?" Fashion Brain Academy, https://fashionbrainacademy.com/what-is-a-trunk-show-and-how-do-i-make-one-work-for-me/.

3. John Middick, "7 Steps to Take Before Accepting Commissions," *Sharpened Artist*, October 29, 2016, https://sharpenedartist.com/cpblog/2016/10/25/7-steps-to-take-before-accepting-commissions.

Chapter 3

1. "Regional vs. National Accreditation—There's a Huge Difference," EDsmart.org, https://www.edsmart.org/regional-vs-national-accreditation/.

2. US Department of Labor, "Apprenticeship Toolkit," https://www.dol.gov/apprenticeship/toolkit/toolkitfaq.htm#1a.

3. US Department of Labor, "Apprenticeship Toolkit: What Are the Basic Program Components of Apprenticeship?" https://www.dol.gov/apprenticeship/toolkit/toolkitfaq.htm#1b.

Chapter 4

1. Steve Jobs, Commencement Address to Stanford University, 2005, https://news.stanford.edu/2005/06/14/jobs-061505/.

2. Anita Campbell, "How to Start a Craft Business," US Small Business Administration, October 31, 2017, https://www.sba.gov/blog/how-start-craft-business.

3. Ibid.

4. Ibid.

5. eHealth, "How Much Does Individual Health Insurance Cost?" June 27, 2019, https://www.ehealthinsurance.com/resources/accident-insurance/how-much-does-individual-health-insurance-cost.

6. Rebecca Lake, "5 Insurance Policies to Buy If You're Self-Employed," Smart Asset, June 11, 2018, https://smartasset.com/career/5-insurance-policies-to-buy-if-youre-self-employed.

7. Arielle O'Shea, "Retirement Plan Options for the Self-Employed," NerdWallet, June 25, 2019, https://www.nerdwallet.com/blog/investing/retirement-plans-self-employed/.

8. Calculator.net, "Retirement Calculator," https://www.calculator.net/retirement-calculator.html.

9. Internal Revenue Service, "Self-Employed Individuals Tax Center," https://www.irs.gov/businesses/small-businesses-self-employed/self-employed-individuals-tax-center.

Glossary

aesthetic: The qualities of how something looks and feels, for instance, "beautiful" is an aesthetic quality.

apprentice: Someone who is learning a craft or trade from a skilled employer, having agreed to work for a fixed period at low wages.

annealer (annealing oven): A kiln used in glassmaking where shaped pieces can cool gradually to prevent brittleness.

artisan: Someone who works in a skilled trade, especially one that involves making things by hand, especially in limited quantities using traditional methods.

balance sheet: A business document that tracks the balance between assets, liabilities, and capital.

blacksmith: Someone who makes things by forging and shaping them out of iron and steel.

carpentry: Making things out of wood, especially unfinished pieces such as framing walls for buildings and roofs.

cash flow: The cash that comes in and out of your business.

casting: Making an object in glass, metal, or other material by pouring the melted (molten) substance into a mold, often of sand or wax.

ceramic artist: An artisan who makes unique objects from ceramic materials that reflect the artisan's personal style.

ceramic engineer: Someone trained in the chemistry and physics of ceramic materials; usually works in industrial ceramics.

ceramics: Things made from materials that change when heated; includes clay, pottery, porcelain, glazes, and related materials.

ceramist: Someone who works with ceramic materials; this could be for artistic or industrial purposes.

clay: A finely grained soil that combines clay minerals that form where there is water. Clay is naturally damp and pliable, so it can be shaped into many different forms. When it dries, it becomes hard and brittle. When fired, it stays hard but is not so brittle.

commission: Contracting for a piece of art or craft to be created according to certain agreed-upon specifications for an agreed-upon amount of money.

consignment: Placing an item with someone else for a specified period of time to be sold by them, while retaining ownership of the item until it is sold.

craft artist: Someone who creates handmade objects, such as pottery, glassware, textiles, and other objects that are designed to be functional.

craft fair: An event where craft artists sell things they have made by hand, usually over a period of a few days.

craftsmanship: Demonstrating skill in a particular craft through the quality of design and work shown in something made by hand.

creativity: Using the imagination or original ideas, especially in the production of an artistic work.

dexterity: The ability to manipulate objects with your hands, especially to manipulate small objects with your fingers.

emerging artist: An artist in the early stage of their career.

entrepreneur: A person who starts a business or businesses and assumes the risks associated with starting a new business.

glassblowing: The technique of shaping glass by blowing air through a tube into a blob of molten glass.

glaze: A powdered mixture of minerals such as premelted glass that is made into a slip and applied to a baked ceramic object by spraying or dipping, which fuses into a glassy coating when dried and fired.

glory hole: The second furnace used in glassblowing, used to reheat pieces between steps in the working process.

hobby: An activity that someone does regularly for pleasure in their leisure time.

internship: A short-term, often low-paid or unpaid position in which someone can learn on the job; an internship should be arranged through a college or trade school and carry some academic credit to balance the lack of pay.

IRA: Individual retirement account.

jewelry: Objects made to decorate the body (such as rings, bracelets, necklaces, earrings, etc.), usually removable, and that may or may not contain jewels.

journeyman: A qualified worker who has learned a trade and works for another person.

jury/jurying/juried: The process of evaluating a craftsperson's or artist's work by experts in the same field.

kiln: A special furnace or oven used for heating clay or glass to high temperatures (i.e., firing).

marketing: Determining who will want to buy your work and the various ways you can use to let them know what you make and how to buy it.

master craftsperson: Someone who has mastered a specific trade or craft, who may employ and train apprentices; today this is usually a status bestowed by a professional association or organization after a jurying process.

median: A value or quantity at the midpoint of a frequency distribution of values or quantities, where there is an equal probability of falling above or below it.

metalsmithing: Making tools, jewelry, or other useful objects out of metal; metalsmithing can use any metal (gold, silver, copper, etc.) and does not have to include forging.

open studio: An event where an artist or craftsperson welcomes visitors into their workspace to see what they make and how they make it.

P&L statement: Profit-and-loss statement or income statement; a business form used to track income and expenses on a quarterly and/or annual basis.

pottery: Making things from clay.

production: Making large quantities of a particular piece.

profession: An activity that someone does to earn a living, particularly one that requires a specific set of skills or body of knowledge.

renaissance: Rebirth.

retail: Selling goods to the public directly.

small business: An independently owned and operated company that is limited in size and revenue, with few or no employees beyond the owner.

stockist: A store or gallery that carries the craft products that artisans make.

studio potter: Someone who makes both unique pieces and sometimes production pottery.

style: The qualities of an artist's or artisan's work that makes it identifiably theirs.

tattoo: An indelible mark or picture made on someone's body by inserting pigment under the skin by means of a needle.

technique: The skills used in a particular craft field.

throwing: Shaping clay on a potter's/throwing wheel.

throwing wheel: A machine with a spinning disk used in the shaping and decorating of round ceramic ware; also called a potter's wheel.

trade show: An exhibition where businesses in a particular industry promote their products and services, usually to other businesses who order goods in large quantities.

trunk show: A sales event where a particular designer, craft artist, or company presents their merchandise to potential customers, usually in a boutique or speciality store.

wholesale: Selling goods (usually in large quantities) to another business that will sell them to the public.

woodworking: Making things out of wood, especially furniture, cabinetry, and other finished pieces.

Resources

This section includes useful resources relating to careers in the craft arts plus information specific to the craft arts covered in this book. Of course, this is not a complete list of all the information out there, but these resources will help you get started finding out more about the craft arts you're interested in.

Craft Arts

American Craft Council
https://craftcouncil.org
This organization supports professional makers with awards, nonprofit shows, conferences, educational resources, the magazine *American Craft,* and other resources.

Craft Gate Art & Craft Directory
http://www.craftgate.com/
This website lists a wide variety of resources for craft artists by medium.

The College Board, Big Future, Career: Craft Artists
https://bigfuture.collegeboard.org/careers/arts-visualand-performing-craft-artists
This site contains useful information and statistics on the craft artist career path.

The Craftsmanship Initiative
https://craftsmanship.net/the-initiative/overview/
According to the website:

> We shine a light on people dedicated to reclaiming craftsmanship's principles of excellence, beauty, and durability as a pathway to a better world.
>
> Our flagship program, launched in 2015, is *Craftsmanship Quarterly,* a multimedia online magazine focusing on in-depth profiles of intriguing artisans and innovators across the globe. We develop partnerships with

organizations that are dedicated to educating and supporting artisans; working toward environmental sustainability; and incorporating craftsmanship into healthy local economies.

Craft Business

The Art Career Project
https://www.theartcareerproject.com

This website provides information for people interested in pursuing careers in certain art and craft fields, including work environment, educational requirements, salary and job prospects, and other useful information. Craft-related pages include:

- Blacksmithing: https://www.theartcareerproject.com/careers/blacksmith/
- Ceramics: https://www.theartcareerproject.com/careers/ceramics/
- Craft Art: https://www.theartcareerproject.com/careers/craft-art/
- Floral Design: https://www.theartcareerproject.com/careers/floral-design/
- Glassblowing: https://www.theartcareerproject.com/careers/glassblowing/
- Metal Fabrication: https://www.theartcareerproject.com/careers/metal -fabrication/
- Tattoo Art: https://www.theartcareerproject.com/careers/tattoo-art/
- Taxidermy: https://www.theartcareerproject.com/careers/taxidermy/
- Woodworking: https://www.theartcareerproject.com/careers/wood working/

Association for Creative Industries
https://craftandhobby.org/eweb/

Formerly the Craft & Hobby Association, this trade association supports the global creative arts products industries through education, events, and membership benefits. ACI hosts the annual Creativation convention.

Craft Fairs Online
http://www.craftsfaironline.com

A directory of crafts-oriented websites that offers organized links to thousands of individual crafters' websites plus craft web malls, crafts organizations, supplies, listings of real world shows, craft publications, instruction, software and more.

Crafts Law

www.craftslaw.com

This website provides introductory information on things like contracts, commissions, patents, insurance, studio rental, and other legal and business issues for the craft artist. This site is published by the staff of attorney Richard Stim's blog: *Dear Rich: An Intellectual Property Blog* (http://dearrichblog.blog spot.com).

Designing an MBA

https://designinganmba.com

This website features courses and articles by designer, metalsmith, educator, and entrepreneur Megan Auman. Topics include wholesale sales, marketing, and other business topics for artist and artisan entrepreneurs.

FestivalNet.com

https://festivalnet.com/

This website features an extensive and comprehensive database of festivals and fairs.

Handmade Business

http://handmade-business.com

A magazine that addresses the business aspects of craft artistry. This is an important source for information about craft trade shows, business advice articles, and webinars.

Heart Hook Home

https://hearthookhome.com

This blog by Ashlea Konecny has tips for people interested in turning craft hobbies into craft businesses.

LiveAboutDotCom

https://www.liveabout.com/

This blog by Marie Loughran has helpful business advice for craft art businesses.

OrderSpace Blog
https://www.orderspace.com/blog/
    OrderSpace is a product for B2B (business-to-business) wholesale ordering. Whether or not you use the program, the company's blog is a wealth of information about working with wholesale customers, trade shows, and more.

US Bureau of Labor Statistics Occupational Outlook Handbook:
   Craft and Fine Artists
https://www.bls.gov/ooh/arts-and-design/craft-and-fine-artists.htm
    This website provides information and quick facts on careers for craft artists and fine artists.

Education and Apprenticeship

American Craft Council, Resources: Schools with Craft Workshops and Courses
https://craftcouncil.org/resources/Schools-with-Craft-Workshops-and-Courses
    The American Craft Council provides many resources, including a state-by-state list of schools that offer craft workshops and courses.

Apprenticeship.gov
http://www.apprenticeship.gov
    This website lets you search for apprenticeships in different fields and different locations.

Apprenticeship Toolkit: Advancing Apprenticeship as a Workforce Strategy
https://www.dol.gov/apprenticeship/toolkit/toolkitfaq.htm#1c
    This website has answers to many, many frequently asked questions about apprenticeships for both apprenticeship-seekers and businesses.

Penland School of Craft
https://penland.org/
    From the school's website:

> Penland School of Craft is an international center for craft education dedicated to helping people live creative lives. Located in the Blue Ridge Mountains of North Carolina, Penland offers one-, two-, and eight-week workshops in books, paper, clay, drawing, glass, iron, metals, photography, printmaking,

letterpress, textiles, and wood. The school also offers artists' residencies, local programs, and a gallery and information center.

Scholarships and Grants, US Community College Scholarships and Grants
http://www.scholarshipsandgrants.us/community-college-scholarships/

ScholarshipPoints.com, Community College Scholarships
https://www.scholarshippoints.com/scholarships/community-college-scholarships/

US Department of Labor, Apprenticeship
https://www.dol.gov/apprenticeship/
This website has information about apprenticeship policy, National Apprenticeship Week, and resources like High School Apprenticeship Programs and Federal Apprenticeship Programs.

US Department of Labor, Apprenticeship Toolkit Frequently Asked Questions
https://www.dol.gov/apprenticeship/toolkit/toolkitfaq.htm#1b
This highly detailed FAQ answers tons of questions about apprenticeships.

Blacksmithing and Metalwork

Artist-Blacksmith's Association of North America (ABANA)
https://abana.org/
From the website:

> The Artist-Blacksmith's Association of North America (ABANA) is dedicated to perpetuating the noble art of blacksmithing. A blacksmith is one who shapes and forges iron with hammer and anvil. ABANA encourages and facilitates the training of blacksmiths; disseminates information about sources of material and equipment; exposes the art of blacksmithing to the public; serves as a center of information about blacksmithing for the general public, architects, interior designers, and other interested parties.—ABANA Mission Statement

ABANA has a wealth of information for beginning and professional blacksmiths, including schools and colleges that teach blacksmithing, publications, discount vendors, educational membership, conferences, awards, and other benefits.

The Anvil's Ring, a quarterly magazine for ABANA members that covers articles, tips, historical notes, photos of members' work, supplier ads, book reviews and event information.

The Hammer's Blow, also a quarterly magazine for ABANA members, has an educational focus and features how-to articles. This magazine is included in ABANA's reduced-rate youth membership.

Ceramics/Pottery

American Art Pottery Association
https://aapa.info/
This organization promotes interest, understanding, appreciation, and recognition of American art pottery through membership benefits, an annual convention, and the *Journal of the American Art Pottery Association*.

American Ceramic Society (ACerS)
https://ceramics.org
This organization is focused on ceramic and glass technologies and industries.

National Council on Education for the Ceramic Arts
https://nceca.net
This nonprofit organization engages and sustains a community for ceramic art, teaching and learning. NCECA provides programing that affects professional artists, K–12 schools, community centers, universities, museums, galleries, businesses, organizations, collectors and enthusiasts of ceramic art.

Glass Art

Art Alliance for Contemporary Glass
https://contempglass.org
This nonprofit organization "whose mission is to further the development and appreciation of art made from glass." Its focus is on collectors, exhibitions, and so on. It provides small scholarships for artists through the Visionary Scholarship Program, as well as grants for exhibitions, catalogs, residencies, and the like for arts organizations.

Association of Clay and Glass Artists of California
https://acga.net/
This and other regional organizations provide opportunities for craft artists to show and sell their work.

Craft Schmaft, Glass Blowing: Complete Beginner's Guide
https://craftschmaft.com/glass-blowing-complete-beginners-guide
This site provides a quick overview of many things a beginning glass artist needs to know.

Glass Art Society
https://www.glassart.org/
This is an international nonprofit organization to "encourage excellence, to advance education, to promote the appreciation and development of the glass arts, and to support the worldwide community of artists who work with glass." It hosts annual conferences and offers members publications and exhibition opportunities, among other resources.

Stained Glass Association of America
https://stainedglass.org
This organization maintains a website that lists professional stained glass studios, manages grants and scholarships, and publishes the *Stained Glass Quarterly*.

Study.com, Schools with Glass Blowing Programs
https://study.com/articles/Schools_with_Glass_Blowing_Programs_How_to
_Choose.html

Jewelry

American School of Jewelry
https://www.jewelryschool.net
This school offers courses in Sunrise, Florida, in jewelry making and design, wax design and casting, stone setting, diamond grading, and CAD design.

Jewelers of America
https://www.jewelers.org/
This is the leading nonprofit jewelry association in the United States. Founded by jewelers, for jewelers to advance the professionalism and ethics

of the jewelry industry. They offer a code of professional practice, education, member benefits, and certifications in sales and management.

Jewelers Board of Trade
http://www.jewelersboard.com
This is a not-for-profit association that provides commercial credit information, collections, marketing services, and unbiased data and statistics on thousands of retail, wholesale and manufacturing jewelers.

Trade Associations and Organizations for Jewelers
http://www.jewelersboard.com/Content.aspx?ID=2057
A list of trade associations and organizations for different kinds of jewelers can be found on this website.

US Bureau of Labor Statistics Occupational Outlook Handbook: Jewelers and Precious Stone and Metal Workers
https://www.bls.gov/ooh/production/jewelers-and-precious-stone-and-metal-workers.htm
This website gives recent data on median pay, entry-level education, job prospects, and other information about jewelry design and jewelry making as a career.

Tattoo Arts

Alliance of Professional Tattooists
www.safe-tattoos.com
This organization addresses health and safety issues in the tattoo industry. It holds an annual tradeshow and exposition for professional tattooists and apprentices with seminars, workshops, and lectures on tattoo techniques, medical issues, first aid, shop security, ethics, and other topics.

Tattoo Artists Guild
www.tattooartistsguild.com
This organization, focused on the tattoo community, encourages member-generated content on its website.

Tattoos.com
http://tattoos.com

This website sponsors international tattoo conventions and lists professional tattoo studios in the United States, Canada, and other countries. The website includes articles, videos, job listings, design ideas, and professional service packages.

Woodworking

American Association of Woodturners
http://www.woodturner.org

This nonprofit organization based in Minnesota provides education, information, and inspiration related to woodturning.

The Furniture Society
http://furnsoc.org

Located in Libertyville, Ilinois, this organization has a national and international membership. According to its website: "Built on a tradition of volunteerism, The Furniture Society works to realize its mission through educational programs, publications, exhibitions, recognition of excellence in the field, and annual conferences."

National Wood Carvers Association
http://chipchats.org

An organization for people who whittle, carve, or sculpt wood.

Woodworkers Guild of America
http://www.wwgoa.com

This organization provides information, ideas, and instruction for woodworkers at all levels. Its website has how-to videos, skill-building articles, and projects for beginners and more advanced woodworkers.

Woodworking Network
http://www.woodworkingnetwork.com

A website for the woodworking community—from individuals through large corporations—including articles and information about technology, supplies, and education, woodworking publications, and community-related content like "Ask a Woodworker," the Craftsman's Challenge contest, and a list of woodworking industry associations.

US Bureau of Labor Statistics Occupational Outlook Handbook: Woodworkers
https://www.bls.gov/ooh/production/woodworkers.htm

This website gives recent data on median pay, entry-level education, job prospects, and other information about woodworking as a career.

Bibliography

American Craft Council. "Resources: Schools with Craft Workshops and Courses." https://craftcouncil.org/resources/Schools-with-Craft-Work shops-and-Courses.

The Art Career Project. "Careers in Art." https://www.theartcareerproject.com/careers/.

Art Design Consultants, LLC. "Artists Are Entrepreneurs: Your Art Is Your Business." *Artwork Archive*. https://www.artworkarchive.com/blog/artists -are-entrepreneurs-your-art-is-your-business.

Association for Creative Industries. "Association for Creative Industries Reveals Size of US Creative Products Opportunity Is $43 Billion," January 22, 2017. http://www.creativationshow.org/media/news-releases/2017/01/27 /association-for-creative-industries-reveals-size-of-us-creative-products -opportunity-is-$43-billion.

Auman, Megan. "Wholesale vs. Consignment." *Designing an MBA*, February 18, 2010. https://designinganmba.com/2010/02/18/wholesale -vs-consignment/.

Calculator.net. "Retirement Calculator." https://www.calculator.net/retirement -calculator.html.

Campbell, Anita. "How to Start a Craft Business." US Small Business Administration, October 31, 2017. https://www.sba.gov/blog/how-start -craft-business.

Chegg CareerMatch. "Career Insights: How Much Does a Tattoo Artist Make?" https://www.careermatch.com/job-prep/career-insights/articles/how -much-does-a-tattoo-artist-make/.

Cogger, Dawn. "How to Be a Craft Fair Vendor." *Untrained Housewife*, October 10, 2010. http://untrainedhousewife.com/how-to-be-a-craft-fair-vendor.

College Board. "Career: Craft Artists." *BigFuture*. https://bigfuture.colleg eboard.org/careers/arts-visualand-performing-craft-artists.

Commonwealth of Massachusetts. "Apprenticeships." https://www.mass.gov /topics/apprenticeships.

Craft Schmaft. "Glass Blowing: Complete Beginner's Guide," December 29, 2018. https://craftschmaft.com/glass-blowing-complete-beginners-guide.

Dillehay, James. "Craft Trade Shows." *CraftMarketer*, March 3, 2017. https://craftmarketer.com/craft-trade-shows/.

EDsmart. "Regional vs. National Accreditation—There's a Huge Difference." https://www.edsmart.org/regional-vs-national-accreditation/.

eHealth. "How Much Does Individual Health Insurance Cost?" June 27, 2019. https://www.ehealthinsurance.com/resources/accident-insurance/how-much-does-individual-health-insurance-cost.

Finch, Carol. "Difference between Internship & Apprenticeship." *Chron*, June 27, 2018. https://work.chron.com/difference-between-internship-apprenticeship-29606.html.

Glover, Richard. "Principles of Great Design: Craftsmanship." *Smashing*, January 13, 2010. https://www.smashingmagazine.com/2010/01/principles-of-great-design-craftsmanship/.

Gungor, Michael. *The Crowd, the Critic and the Muse: A Book for Creators.* Denver, CO: Woodsley Press, 2012.

Hammill, Jane. "What Is a Trunk Show and How Do I Make One Work for Me?" Fashion Brain Academy. https://fashionbrainacademy.com/what-is-a-trunk-show-and-how-do-i-make-one-work-for-me/.

Handmade Business. "Craft Show Listings." http://handmade-business.com/craft-show-listings/.

Hudson, Matthew. "The 15 Steps to Open a Retail Store." The Balance Small Business, April 23, 2018. https://www.thebalancesmb.com/retail-4161588.

Hunter, Dan. "Tattoo Artist Salaries—How Much Do Tattoo Artists Earn?" AuthorityTattoo. https://authoritytattoo.com/how-much-do-tattoo-artists-make/.

Internal Revenue Service. "Self-Employed Individuals Tax Center." https://www.irs.gov/businesses/small-businesses-self-employed/self-employed-individuals-tax-center.

Jobs, Steve. Commencement Address to Stanford University, 2005. https://news.stanford.edu/2005/06/14/jobs-061505/.

Josephson, Amelia. "The Economics of Craft Fairs." SmartAsset, August 20, 2018. https://smartasset.com/career/the-economics-of-craft-fairs.

Kelly Services. "Nine Tips for Improving Your Interpersonal Skills." https://www.kellyservices.ca/ca/careers/career-resource-centre/managing-your-career/nine-tips-for-improving-your-interpersonal-skills/.

Kiersey, David. "Portrait of an Artisan." The Kiersey Group. https://keirsey
.com/temperament/artisan-overview/.

Konecny, Ashlea. "18 Craft Fair Tips for Beginners: How to Run a Successful Craft
Show Booth." *Heart Hook Home*, March 7, 2017. https://hearthookhome
.com/beginners-craft-fair-tips-how-to-run-a-successful-craft-show-booth/.

Lake, Rebecca. "5 Insurance Policies to Buy If You're Self-Employed."
SmartAsset, June 11, 2018. https://smartasset.com/career/5-insurance
-policies-to-buy-if-youre-self-employed.

Lovering, Catherine. "How to Be Successful Selling Your Artwork and Crafts."
http://smallbusiness.chron.com/successful-selling-artwork-crafts-251
97.html.

Loughran, Maire. "The Five Types of Crafts: Textile, Decorative, Paper,
Functional, and Fashion Crafts." LiveAboutDotCom, January 21, 2019.
https://www.liveabout.com/the-five-types-of-crafts-193034.

———. "10 Steps to Follow before You Start a Crafts Business."
LiveAboutDotCom, June 10, 2018. https://www.liveabout.com/steps
-before-you-start-crafts-business-193036.

———. "The Three Types of Arts and Crafts Businesses: Service, Merchandising
and Manufacturing Companies." LiveAboutDotCom, March 31, 2019.
https://www.liveabout.com/three-types-of-arts-crafts-businesses-192760.

———. "The 3 Types of Financial Statements: Income Statement, Balance Sheet,
and Statement of Cash Flows." LiveAboutDotCom, April 18, 2018. https://
www.liveabout.com/the-three-types-of-financial-statements-192716.

Meyer, Aurora. "Becoming a Craftsman Entrepreneur." *Dispatches from the
Castle*, September 19, 2016. https://aurorameyer.com/2016/09/19/becom
ing-a-craftsman-entrepreneur/.

Middick, John. "7 Steps to Take before Accepting Commissions." *Sharpened
Artist*, October 29, 2016. https://sharpenedartist.com/cpblog/2016/10/25
/7-steps-to-take-before-accepting-commissions.

Oppenheimer, Todd, and the Craftsmanship Initiative Team. The Crafsmanship
Initiative. https://craftsmanship.net/the-initiative/overview/.

O'Shea, Arielle. "Retirement Plan Options for the Self-Employed." Nerd
Wallet, June 25, 2019. https://www.nerdwallet.com/blog/investing/retire
ment-plans-self-employed/.

Perrin, Christopher. "The Apprenticeship Model: A Journey toward Mastery."
Intro to ClassicalU, January 12, 2017. https://www.classicalu.com
/the-apprenticeship-model-three-levels-to-mastery/.

Peterson, Beth. "The Difference between Pottery and Ceramics." The Spruce Crafts, April 21, 2019. https://www.thesprucecrafts.com/what-are-pot tery-and-ceramics-2745954.

Pilon, Annie. "25 Places to Sell Handmade Crafts Online." Small Business Trends, February 7, 2019. https://smallbiztrends.com/2015/06/places-to -sell-handmade-crafts-online.html.

Resnick, Rosalind. "How to Sell at Craft Fairs and Shows." Entrepreneur. https://www.entrepreneur.com/article/76936.

Rothfuss, Patrick. The Wise Man's Fear (Kingkiller Chronicle #2). New York: DAW Books, 2011.

Schmidlkofer, C. M. "How to Get Commissioned Work as a Craft Artist." Handmade Business. http://handmade-business.com/how-to-get-commis sioned-work-as-a-craft-artist/.

ScholarshipPoints. "Community College Scholarships." https://www.scholar shippoints.com/scholarships/community-college-scholarships/.

Stim, Richard. CraftsLaw. https://www.craftslaw.com/.

Tiffany, Laura. "Starting an Arts & Crafts Business." Entrepreneur, April 1, 2002. https://www.entrepreneur.com/article/50544.

Truity Psychometrics. "Craft or Fine Artist." https://www.truity.com/career -profile/craft-or-fine-artist.

US Bureau of Labor Statistics. "Craft and Fine Artists." https://www.bls.gov/ooh /arts-and-design/craft-and-fine-artists.htm.

US Department of Labor. "Apprenticeship." https://www.dol.gov /apprenticeship/.

———. "Apprenticeship Toolkit." https://www.dol.gov/apprenticeship/tool kit/toolkitfaq.htm#1a.

Vicki. "How to Approach New Stockists." OrderSpace, December 12, 2017. https://www.orderspace.com/blog/approaching-new-stockists/.

Weisser, Cybele. "Jobs for People Who Love Doing Crafts." Monster.com. https://www.monster.com/career-advice/article/5-great-jobs-people -love-doing-crafts-0323.

Wood, Robin. "Apprenticeships in Traditional Crafts," January 5, 2010. http://www.robin-wood.co.uk/woodcraft-blog/2010/01/05/apprentice ships-in-traditional-crafts/.

About the Author

Marcia Santore is a writer and artist from New England. She enjoys writing about interesting people and the fascinating stuff they do. She's written on many topics, including profiles of artists, scholars, scientists, and business people. She has also illustrated and published several children's books. See her writing website at www.amalgamatedstory.com. See her own artwork at www .marciasantore.com. Read her interviews with artists on her blog *artYOP!* at www.artyop.com.